YOU & SELF-ESTEEM:
IT'S THE KEY TO HAPPINESS & SUCCESS
(A Self-Esteem Workbook for Grades 5-12)

By Bettie B. Youngs, Ph.D.

JP

JALMAR PRESS
ROLLING HILLS ESTATES, CALIFORNIA

YOU & SELF-ESTEEM:
The Key To Happiness & Sucess
(A Self-Esteem Workbook for Grades 5-12)

Copyright © 1992 by Bettie B. Youngs, Ph.D.

All rights reserved. No part of this work may be reproduced by any mechanical, photographic, or electronic process, or in the form of a photographic recording, nor may it be stored in a retrieval system, transmitted or otherwise copied for public or private use without the written permission of the publisher. Requests for permission should be addressed to:

>Jalmar Press
>Permissions Dept.
>45 Hitching Post Drive, Bldg. 2
>Rolling Hills Estates, CA 90274
>(310) 547-1240 FAX: (310) 547-1644

Library of Congress Cataloging-in-Publication Data:

Youngs, Bettie B.
    You & self-esteem: The key to happiness & success (A self-esteem workbook for grades 5-12) / by Bettie B. Youngs.
       p. cm.
    Includes bibliographical references
    Summary: A practical workbook that emphasizes the importance of self-esteem and how it can be developed and nourished. Includes exercises, quizzes, and questions for thought.
    ISBN 0-915190-83-4 : $16.95
    1. Self-respect — Juvenile literature. 2. Self-perception — Juvenile literature.
    3. Success — Psychological aspects — Juvenile literature.
    [1. Self-respect.] I. Title II. Title: You and self-esteem.
BF697.5. S46Y68 1992   91-058825
158 — dc20   **CIP**

20+YEARS
AWARD WINNING PUBLISHER

Published by Jalmar Press

YOU & SELF-ESTEEM:
The Key to Happiness & Success
(A Self-Esteem Workbook for Grades 5-12)

Written by: Bettie B. Youngs
Edited by: Marie Ciconte
Production Consultant: Charles E. Simpson
Book Coordination & Cover Design by: Jeanne Duke
Typography by: Mario A. Artavia II
Manufactured in the United States of America

First edition printing: 10 9 8 7 6 5 4 3 2 1

About The Author

Bettie B. Youngs, Ph. D. is an internationally known lecturer, author, counselor and consultant. Her work has spanned more than 60 countries for more than two decades, earning her a reputation as a respected authority in the field of personal and professional effectiveness. She has earned national acclaim for her work on the effects of stress on health, wellness and productivity for both adults and children, and for her work on the role of self-esteem as it detracts from or empowers vitality, achievement and peak performance. Dr. Youngs has conducted extensive research on the stages of growth and development in the K-12 years and their implications for program and curriculum development.

Bettie is a former Teacher-of-the-Year, Professor at San Diego State University, Executive Director of the Phoenix Foundation, and currently serves as a consultant to U.S. schools. She is the author of 14 books published in 23 languages, as well as a number of popular audio cassette programs.

Dr. Youngs, a member of the National Speakers Association, addresses audiences throughout the U.S. and abroad, and meets with nearly 250,000 youth and adults each year. She serves on the Board of Directors for the National Council for Self-Esteem and is a frequent guest on radio and television talk shows. A leader in U.S. education, her consulting firm provides instruction and professional development to school districts nationwide. She may be contacted at:

Bettie B. Youngs & Associates
Instruction & Professional Development, Inc.
3060 Racetrack View Drive
Del Mar, CA 92014
(619) 481-6360

Other Works By Bettie B. Youngs, Ph.D.

BOOKS:

Stress In Children (New York: Avon Books, 1985)

Helping Your Teenager Deal With Stress (New York: Tarcher/St. Martins Press, 1986)

A Stress Management Guide For Young People (Rolling Hills Estates, CA: Jalmar Press, 1986)

Is Your Net-Working? A Complete Guide to Building Contacts and Career Visibility (New York: John Wiley & Sons, 1989)

Friendship Is Forever, Isn't It? (Rolling Hills Estates, CA: Jalmar Press, 1990)

Goal Setting Skills for Young Adults (Rolling Hills Estates, CA: Jalmar Press, 1990)

Getting Back Together: Creating a New Relationship With Your Partner and Making it Last (New York: Bob Adams, Inc., 1990)

Problem Solving Skills For Children (Rolling Hills Estates, CA: Jalmar Press, 1990)

A Stress Management Guide for Administrators (Rolling Hills Estates, CA: Jalmar Press, 1993)

The 6 Vital Ingredients of Self-Esteem: How to Develop Them in Your Child (New York: MacMillan/Rawson, 1991)

The 6 Vital Ingredients of Self-Esteem: How to Develop Them in Your Students (Rolling Hills Estates, CA: Jalmar Press, 1992)

Stress Management For Educators (Rolling Hills Estates, CA: Jalmar Press, 1992)

Enhancing The Educator's Self-Esteem: It's Your Criteria #1 (Rolling Hills Estates, CA: Jalmar Press, 1992)

AUDIO CASSETTES:

Helping Your Teenager Deal With Stress (Rolling Hills Estates, CA: Jalmar Press, 1987)

How to Raise Happy, Healthy, Self-Confident Children (Nightengale/Conant, 1990)

The 6 Vital Components of Self-Esteem and How To Develop Them In Your Child (Sybervision, 1990)

Helping Children Manage Stress, Pressure, and Anxiety (Sybervision, 1991)

Developing Responsibility in Children (Sybervision, 1991)

Getting Back Together (Sybervision, 1991)

YOU & SELF-ESTEEM:
It's the Key to Happiness & Success

By Bettie B. Youngs, Ph.D.

WHAT OTHERS ARE SAYING ABOUT THIS BOOK:

"The relationship between a young person's self-esteem and his discovering and fulfilling potential is undeniable. This well-written, thoroughly enjoyable, and comprehensive book helps young people themselves examine the vital ingredients essential to high self-esteem, and provides the skills necessary in helping them value and nourish their self-esteem. This is a landmark book in personal development for the student."
Robert Lockwood, Principal, Denver, Colorado

"Getting young people to participate in the goal to become all they are capable of becoming is a matter of *self-esteem*. This book, developed for young people themselves, gets at the heart of helping young people do that."
Marilyn Keppler, High School Educator, Binghamton, New York

"Students with high self-esteem often excel *beyond* our expectations. I've always associated a student's inner sense of self — what Dr. Youngs would call 'the student's reputation with himself' — as his baseline for performance. A student's level of self-esteem is a better predictor of school achievement and life success than IQ or grades. This book is about providing young people with the information and skills they need to build a positive self-esteem, to overcome a shattered one, and to design healthy patterns workable in school and personal life. This book should be a required course in *every* school."
Terry Van de Camp, Junior High Teacher, Augusta, Georgia

"A student's self-esteem is central to his being a well-adjusted student, and to his ability to learn. This book enables young people to succeed in school and in life. It's a great book — a real break-through for our young people."
Marjorie Little, Middle School Educator, Seattle, Washington

"This book is about empowering young people with a sense of self-mastery so that they feel capable in developing their talents and aptitudes. Each chapter provides important information on developing one's self-esteem, anecdotes that students can relate to, and a full compliment of motivational skills and tools helping young people manifest high self-esteem. This book should be required reading in every middle school and high school."
Jan Christiansen, Counselor, Iowa City, Iowa

"When I learned that my self-esteem was MINE to care for, I began to take better care of myself. There are so many things that I'm asked to do by others. But my self-esteem is mine; I get to decide how to treat me. I've learned that how I do that is directly related to how others will treat me."
Maryann Olds, 8th grader, Fort Worth, Texas

"I used to think of growing up as 'what I was going to **do**'; after going through this self-esteem course, I think more in terms of 'what I want to **be**.'"
Denny Dobran, 9th grader, Salt Lake City, Utah

"This book gave me back *me*. I used to think that everyone else was in charge of my life, but they aren't. I am. Now I see my parents and teachers as helping me rather than controlling me — or as Dr. Youngs would say, 'They're on your team, but you're the coach.' I like that idea! Basically, I'm responsible for what I will make of my life. It feels great to know that I can care enough about myself to make something of my life."
Tammy Bowman, 10th grader, Des Moines, Iowa

"I was really feeling down on myself because my life looked so rotten. I thought, 'I don't deserve this!' But this book showed me that while some people in my life refused to be there for me, it's still up to me to construct a life and lifestyle for me. I can be good *with* me and *for* me when others aren't. I can also teach others *how* to support me in my dreams and look for those who will. I've also learned to really appreciate my step-dad because he is so good to me and so supportive of me. It may not look like it to others, but I will succeed. No one gets to beat up on my self-esteem any longer — I'm going to be good *to me — and to others*."
Brad Marshall, 11th grader, Lansing, Michigan

"Other kids think that because I get good grades, I've got it made. But I never felt that I was a good student, and often I felt just plain dumb. After reading this book, I decided it was a matter of *my* self-esteem. The *way* I was feeling about myself was actually coming true. When I decided to stop talking negatively to myself and instead to do what Dr. Youngs said, 'to develop an inner language of encouragement,' I not only stopped feeling dumb, but getting good grades was easier."
Noreen Nicole, 9th grader, San Diego, California

To my lovely daughter Jennifer, and to all
the young people I've worked with over the years

A Note From the Author: The terms *he and she* have intentionally been interchanged throughout this text so that you can personalize and relate the material to yourself.

Table Of Contents

INTRODUCTION 1
Is Your Self-Esteem in "Shape"? 3
    The Self-Esteem Fitness Profile for Young Adults 5

UNIT I: THE ALL IMPORTANT SELF-ESTEEM 9
Chapter 1 What Is Self-Esteem? 10
    Self-Esteem — A Definition 10
    How Do You Gain a Healthy Self-Esteem? 11
    The Six Ingredients of Self-Esteem 11
    Characteristics of High Self-Esteem 12
    To Do 13
    To Think About 14

Chapter 2 You Wear Your Self-Esteem 15
    Your (Self-Esteem) Attitude Is Showing 15
    Gerry and Miles 15
    To Do 16
    To Think About 18

Chapter 3 "Testing, Testing!" How's Your Self-Esteem? 19
    How's Your Self-Esteem? 19
    Self-Esteem Is a Day-by-Day Occurrence 19
    Amy's Day 19
    Amy's Rating 21
    Description of Your Day 22
    To Do 23
    To Think About 24

UNIT II: PHYSICAL SAFETY 25
Chapter 4 Physical Safety: Do You Feel Safe at School? 26
    The First Prerequisite: Physical Safety 26
    Do You Feel Safe at School? 26
    Trinh's Story 27
    Darlene's Story 27
    Judson's Story 27
    Sam's Story 27
    Feeling Safe at School 28
    What You Can Do to Feel Safe at School 28
    To Do 30
    To Think About 31

Chapter 5 Physical Safety: Do You Feel Safe at Home and in Your Neighborhood? 32
    Safety in Your Home and Neighborhood 32
    What's Your Home Life Like? 32
    Jessica's Story 32
    Sexual Abuse 34
    Safety in Your Neighborhood 34

- Gwen's Story 34
- Aaron's Story 34
- To Do 35
- To Think About 35

Chapter 6 Physical Safety: Who's In Charge — You or Drugs? 36
- Be Powerful Enough to Just Say No! 36
- "Lucky" Jay 36
- Free From Drugs and Alcohol 37
- "But It's Only a Cigarette!" 37
- To Do 38
- To Think About 39

Chapter 7 Physical Safety: Are You Taking Care of Your Body? 40
- You Count on Your Body (For Life) 40
- Kimberly and Denise 40
- How to Improve Your Health 41
- Setting Lifelong Patterns in Your Diet 41
- Exercise Can Give You Energy 41
- To Do 42
- To Think About 43

UNIT III: EMOTIONAL SECURITY 45

Chapter 8 Emotional Security: What Tune (Message) Is Playing in Your Head? 46
- What Are You Telling Yourself? 46
- Ricardo's Story 46
- Whitney's Story 47
- Are You a Sissy or a Ferrari? 47
- Empowering Your Inner Language 49
- What to Do About Negative Self-Talk 49
- Paul's Story 49
- Changing Unwanted Thoughts 50
- Thought-Stopping 50
- Rewriting Negative Messages 51
- To Do 51
- To Think About 52

Chapter 9 Emotional Security: What Do You Get Stressed Out About? 53
- Understanding Fears and Anxieties 53
- George's Story 53
- You Can Learn to Manage Your Stress 54
- What Is Stress? 54
- Evan and James 55
- Everyone Fears Something: What Causes You Stress? 55
- How Does Stress Affect You? 57
- How Do You Cope With Your Stress? 58
- The Stress Cycle 59
- Rob's Day 59
- To Do 60
- To Think About 62

UNIT IV: IDENTITY 63

Chapter 10 How Unique Do You Think You Really Are? 64
The Nature of Being a Person 64
The Work of Growing Up 64
Stages and Their Tasks 65
To Do 68
To Think About 69

Chapter 11 Identity: Answering the "Who Am I?" Question 70
Uncovering the Real You 70
What Is Your Identity? 71
The Actual, Ideal, and Public Selves 71
Who Are You? 72
The Importance of Appearance 73
How Your Body Image Affects Your Self-Esteem 74
Building a Positive Sense of Identity 74
To Do 75
To Think About 77

Chapter 12 Identity: How Much Are You Influenced by Others? 78
The Influence of Others on Your Self-Esteem 78
Colleen's Story 78
Do You Stand Up for Yourself? 79
To Do 80
To Think About 82

UNIT V: BELONGING 83

Chapter 13 Belonging: Your Need for Friendships 84
Strive for Inderdependence 84
What Groups Do You Belong to? 84
"Basketball Bill" 85
Ending Relationships 86
Skills for Ending Friendships 87
Julie and Ron 87
To Do 88
To Think About 89

Chapter 14 Belonging: Popularity Is About Friendships 90
How Well Do You Get Along With Others? 90
The New Boy in Town: Roger's Story 90
Gene's Story 91
Keys to Popularity 91
What It Takes to Be a Friend 92
To Do 93
To Think About 95

UNIT VI: COMPETENCE 97

Chapter 15 Competence: Do You Feel Capable? 98
Be Willing to Try New Things 98
How Self-Esteem Affects Your Performance 98

- Nick's Story 99
- Don't Be Afraid of Making Mistakes — Here's Why..............................99
- Solving Problems, Generating Alternatives, and Evaluating Consequences 100
- To Do 103
- To Think About 104

Chapter 16 Competence: School as Your World of Work 105
- Feeling Capable in Your "Workplace" 105
- High Self-Esteem Students Fare Better in School 105
- School Is a Tough Career, Even for Good Students 106
- To Do 107
- To Think About 108

UNIT VII: MISSION 109

Chapter 17 Mission: What Makes Your Life Meaningful? 110
- A Purpose Gives Life Zest 110
- Feeling Purposeful Means Taking Responsibility 110
- Responsibility Isn't Always Easy (or Fun)! 111
- Setting and Achieving (Worthwhile) Goals 111
- Being in Charge of Your Life 112
- Are Goals Really All That Important? 112
- Count on Obstacles Along the Way 113
- Seven Steps to Goal Setting 114
- To Do 116
- To Think About 117

Chapter 18 Mission: Setting Goals Is the Key 118
- Life Is a Do-It-Yourself Project 118
- Focus on Your Area of Excellence 118
- How Can You Tell What You Are Good at? 118
- Finding Your Acres of Diamonds 119
- Exercise 1: Identifying Your Acres of Diamonds 120
- Exercise 2: Finding Your Area of Excellence 120
- Exercise 3: Determining Your Number One Goal 121
- Exercise 4: Setting Subgoals 122
- Overcoming Obstacles/Removing the Barriers 123
- To Do 124
- To Think About 125

Chapter 19 Mission: Putting It All Together 126
- Living Life With a Purpose 126
- Keys to Success 126
- The Person Staring Back From the Glass 127
- To Do 128
- To Think About 130

It Begins With You: A Message From the Author 131
- Liking Yourself Is the Key to Liking Others 131

RESOURCES AND SUGGESTED READINGS 133

HELP ORGANIZATIONS 138

NOTES TO REMEMBER 142

INTRODUCTION

Self-Esteem. We hear so much about the importance of self-esteem, but what is it? What makes a healthy or high self-esteem? What tears it down or erodes it? Can others diminish your self-esteem, or are you completely in charge of the way you feel about yourself?

What is the relationship between self-esteem and feeling confident? Why is it that when you feel better about yourself, your life seems to go better overall? How does having a high self-esteem help you become a better student, friend, and learner? How does it spark your desire to set and achieve goals? In what ways does it contribute to your willingness to take responsibility for yourself, to be sensitive to the needs and feelings of your family and friends, to be concerned about your community and what's going on in the world?

Why does the possession of a positive self-esteem lead to inner harmony and an outward reflection of happiness? How does it contribute to your attracting friends with a healthy sense of self-esteem? Why is it that when your self-esteem is low you seem to attract others whose self-esteem is low? How can a positive self-esteem help you to live up to your full potential, to become all you can be?

Those are big questions, and important ones. Looking to your self-esteem as a key to finding the answers is a step in the right direction. The level, health, and vitality of your self-esteem has a strong and definite effect on your accomplishments, your happiness, and the quality of your relationships. Self-esteem is also an important ingredient in how energized you feel. In fact, you might think of it as your battery pack. When your battery is positively charged, you have confidence in yourself, knowing you have "the power" to accomplish anything you set your mind to. You feel capable, worthwhile, and deserving of happiness and love. But when your self-esteem battery is low, even small problems can be a drain on your energy. You are much more preoccupied with your problems (even the little ones seem overwhelming) and less willing to help others. You project an image of insecurity and unhappiness.

Luckily, your self-esteem battery can be recharged. This book is your guide in doing that. By reading, digesting, and working through the exercises in this workbook you will:

- understand what self-esteem is and what it isn't;
- be able to identify why and how self-esteem empowers or detracts from your having the life you really want;
- be able to protect your self-esteem from being shattered by others (and avoid lowering it yourself!); and,
- develop the skills that build and nurture your self-esteem as well as that of others.

Your self-esteem is the key to becoming the positive, achieving, happy, and self-confident person you want to be. With a high self-esteem, you can plan and live an exciting and meaningful life.

I welcome this opportunity to help you discover more about yourself and to learn ways of nourishing your self-esteem.

— Bettie B. Youngs

INTRODUCTION

IS YOUR SELF-ESTEEM IN "SHAPE"?

A SELF-ESTEEM FITNESS PROFILE

THE SELF-ESTEEM FITNESS PROFILE FOR YOUNG ADULTS

© 1992 Bettie B. Youngs, Ph.D.

Maybe you haven't spent too much time thinking about your self-esteem, but it's important that you do. Just like you need to care for your physical body, you need to know if your self-esteem is healthy and fit. Is your self-esteem working for you or against you? The following assessment can help you decide. It's designed to help you examine six key areas in your life and the experiences in each that account for how you feel about yourself. Keep in mind this is not a test; there are no "right" or "wrong" answers — no high or low scores. Think of this assessment as an opportunity for you to get to know yourself a little better.

Read each of the following statements, then circle **T** for true or **F** for false to indicate whether this is an accurate or inaccurate description of yourself. Don't think about each statement too long, or try to analyze it. Just go with your first response. Answer each question based on how you feel most of the time, not on how you feel during particularly good or bad days. This exercise will take about 15 minutes to complete.

EXAMPLE: I get nervous when I have to give a report in front of the class.

If you get nervous when you have to give a report in front of the class, circle **T** for true.

If you do not get nervous when you have to give a report in front of the class, circle **F** for false.

PHYSICAL SAFETY

T F 1. I like the neighborhood I live in; I feel safe there.
T F 2. I like my home, and always feel safe there.
T F 3. I like the school I go to; I always feel safe there.
T F 4. I'm not afraid of any student at school.
T F 5. I seldom go to the nurse's office because of a headache or stomachache.
T F 6. I always make wise choices for the health of my body.
T F 7. I have a healthy, strong, and fit body.
T F 8. My parents discipline fairly.
T F 9. I feel safe when I am at school.
T F 10. I'm not afraid of anyone in my neighborhood.

EMOTIONAL SECURITY

T F 1. I am a self-confident person.
T F 2. I am able to laugh at my own mistakes.
T F 3. It helps to talk about my feelings.

T F 4. I am my own best friend.
T F 5. I expect good things to happen to me.
T F 6. When I mess up, I just try to do it right the next time.
T F 7. I give myself credit when I do something well.
T F 8. I do not think it's important to do everything well.
T F 9. I try never to make fun of others and tease them unfairly.
T F 10. I know how to manage stress and pressure.

IDENTITY, SELFHOOD

T F 1. I am a happy person.
T F 2. I seldom wish I could be someone else.
T F 3. I like the way I look.
T F 4. I like who I am.
T F 5. I like my body.
T F 6. I rarely think that if I had more money and things (like new CDs or more clothes) I would be a lot happier and have more friends.
T F 7. I take care of my appearance, trying to look my best every day.
T F 8. When something good happens to me, I feel I deserve it.
T F 9. I feel comfortable in most situations, even new ones.
T F 10. I often compliment others.

BELONGING, AFFILIATION

T F 1. I have at least two best friends.
T F 2. Other people are willing to give me help when I need it.
T F 3. Whenever I say I will do something, people know I can be counted on.
T F 4. When good things happen to my friends, I'm happy for them.
T F 5. I like most of the people I know, even if we aren't good friends.
T F 6. I'm able to pal around with whom I want; I can pick and choose my friends.
T F 7. Not all my friends are like me.
T F 8. I'm not intimidated by those who tease me and make fun of me.
T F 9. My friends know they can count on me for compliments when they have new clothes or have done something well.
T F 10. Others want to include me in what they are doing.

COMPETENCE

T F 1. I believe people who set goals get what they want out of life.
T F 2. I know how to set priorities and manage my time.
T F 3. I'm smart enough to do what I want when I put my mind to it.
T F 4. I ask others for help when I need it.
T F 5. I take my problems one step at a time.
T F 6. I can make wise choices and good decisions.
T F 7. I listen to the other person's point of view before I decide what to say.
T F 8. When I have trouble paying attention, I just refocus.
T F 9. I don't feel that I always have to do well in everything; sometimes giving it my best is enough.
T F 10. I feel capable of coping with life's challenges.

MISSION, PURPOSE

T F 1. I often think about my future and what it will be like.
T F 2. My life has meaning and direction.
T F 3. Whether I succeed or fail is up to me.
T F 4. I know that I'm going to get what I want out of life.
T F 5. I know what I want to do with my life.
T F 6. I've thought about what I want out of life.
T F 7. I am excited about my present life and look forward to my future.
T F 8. I've thought about what kind of a lifestyle I want to live.
T F 9. There are a lot of things I'm interested in.
T F 10. I have goals, and I'm going to achieve them.

Scoring the Self-Esteem Profile

Perhaps you noticed that the statements in each of the six categories were designed to get **TRUE** responses. To take a look at your overall ratings, count the number of total **FALSE** responses. How many did you have?

Now look at each category separately. More than three **F** responses in any single category represents an area contributing to low self-esteem and a source of problems for you. As you work through this book, pay particular attention to the corresponding chapters that discuss those areas where you had a number of **F** responses. This will help you think about how you can make adjustments or changes in your life, or find out where to turn for help so that you can increase your self-esteem.

Okay, let's begin!

UNIT I

THE ALL IMPORTANT SELF-ESTEEM

CHAPTER 1

WHAT IS SELF-ESTEEM?

Self-Esteem — A Definition

No doubt you've heard the term *self-esteem*. It's used more and more these days because we realize how important self-esteem is in our lives and to our overall well-being. Self-esteem is how much you value yourself. It's your price tag, so to speak. YOU decide if you are valuable merchandise, a markdown, or a reject.

Have you ever noticed how some young people believe they are important and valuable, while others don't seem to think too much of themselves? Have you also noticed that the value each person holds for himself is how others treat him, too? One reason for these differences is the way each individual chooses to think of himself. In other words, the person with healthy self-esteem assigns a high value to his being, his personhood, his life. Now, that's not to say that someone who thinks he's better than someone else is, or that someone who doesn't believe he is special isn't, but rather, that what we choose to believe is an important determinant in the responses we get from other people.

We will examine what a healthy self-esteem is and what it isn't as we go along in this book. But for now, know that self-esteem is your perceived self-value. A story about a boy who came home crying because a classmate had called him a sissy shows how we can choose the way we see ourselves.

"Why are you crying?" his Grandma asked.

"Because Paul called me a sissy! Do you think I'm a sissy, Grandma?" the little boy asked, tears streaming down his face.

"Oh no," said the grandmother. "I think you're a Ferrari."

"What?" said the boy, trying to make sense of what his grandmother had said. "Why do you think I'm a car?"

"Well, if you believe because Paul called you a sissy, that you are, you might as well believe you're a car, and a terrific one at that. Why be a sissy when you can be a Ferrari!"

"Oh," exclaimed the boy gleefully, feeling quite relieved. "I get to decide what I am!"

This simple story illustrates what we all need to believe: Why be a sissy when you can be a Ferrari! We can each *choose* to have a positive and healthy self-esteem.

If you don't believe that you are worthy of happiness, good health, friendship, love, achievement, and success, you may never live your life in a way that can help you become all that you are capable of being. You may never get what you want or need. On the other hand, if you believe in your own worth, you can achieve and succeed!

How Do You Gain a Healthy Self-Esteem?

You don't just wake up one day with a bad or a good self-esteem, or with a high or a low self-esteem. It's developed over time. You earn a healthy self-esteem by actively participating in your life in a meaningful way. For example, you promise to be your own best friend, to always stick by yourself in good times and bad. You take responsibility for your choices, actions, and behavior. You work toward those goals that are important to you. You actively work to change those things that aren't working well for you. You live your life according to a plan that you yourself have devised and approved.

THE SIX INGREDIENTS OF SELF-ESTEEM

Self-esteem is self-regard. Your perception of your worth is the essence of self-esteem. There are six key areas that shape your sense of self-worth. I'll help you examine each of these and look at what they mean in the following chapters, but in a nutshell, these six powerful ingredients of self-esteem are:

1. A Sense of Physical Safety: Feeling physically safe means that you aren't fearful of being harmed or hurt. You feel safe — in your school, home, and neighborhood. You care for your body, knowing that you must protect yourself from anything that could put your health in jeopardy (such as danger, drugs, and alcohol or other substances, and so on).

2. A Sense of Emotional Security: When you know you won't be put down or made to feel less worthy, and when you feel you can confront and deal with your fears, you feel emotionally secure. You feel secure that others won't beat you up emotionally with sarcasm or hurtful words (and that includes things you say to yourself!). You are respectful, considerate, and friendly — to yourself and others. You believe that as a human being you have worth, and you feel deserving of other people's care.

3. A Sense of Identity: Knowing yourself, self-knowledge, allows you to develop a realistic and healthy sense of individuality. You are friends with the face in the mirror, able to "knock, and find somebody (yourself) home." You've taken the time to get to know and understand yourself. In turn, knowing and accepting yourself allows you to care about others. You treat yourself with respect and want others to respect you in return.

4. A Sense of Belonging: When you feel accepted, liked, appreciated, and respected by others, you show respect and acceptance in return. You want to make friends, and you work for harmony in your relationships. While you stand up for yourself, you don't ignore the opinions of others — you are willing to hear them out. But you don't depend on their views to make your decisions. You cannot be easily swayed into making choices that are out of line with what you know to be right for you. In other words, you strive for *interdependence*.

5. A Sense of Competence: Feeling capable gives you the motivation to achieve. When you feel sure of yourself and your abilities, you feel in charge of your life. You feel capable of coping with the challenges in your life. You're willing to try new things, to develop and expand your abilities, to persevere rather than give up when a situation becomes difficult. You're aware of your strengths, and while you also know of those areas where you are less capable, you lead with your strengths.

6. A Sense of Purpose: To feel purposeful you set and achieve goals that are important to you. You know your values and are living your life according to those values. Your values are reflected in your behaviors, and your actions are a reflection of your values. Life has meaning and direction. Life is fun and worthwhile.

When you see yourself as capable and competent, loving and lovable, responsible and caring, you have "high self-esteem." Far from being conceited or self-centered, people with healthy self-esteem have a realistic awareness of themselves, and of their abilities and needs. Because you respect yourself, you are unwilling to allow others to devalue your worth. Just as you won't tear others down, you won't let them tear you down. You care about your well-being, and it shows.

Characteristics of High Self-Esteem

By now you realize that having a healthy self-esteem is very important. Below are listed a few of the many benefits of having a high self-esteem:

- The higher your self-esteem, the better able you are to cope with the ups and downs of your life.

- The higher your self-esteem, the more likely you are to think about what you want out of life, the more ambitious you are in going after it, and the more likely you are to achieve it.

- The higher your self-esteem, the better able you will be to attract others who enjoy their lives and are working to their potentials. Individuals with low self-esteem tend to seek low self-esteem friends who also think poorly of themselves.

- The higher your self-esteem, the more likely you will treat others with respect and fairness, since self-respect is the basis of respect for others.

- The higher your self-esteem, the more you will confront obstacles and fears rather than avoid them. Low self-esteem individuals see problems as grounds for quitting and often say to themselves, "I give up."

- The higher your self-esteem, the better able you will be in finding ways to get along well with others. You strive to be useful, helpful, and responsive.

- The higher your self-esteem, the more compassion you will show for yourself and for others. Compassion exposes self-worth: When you have discovered the treasured value of your personhood, you care about the value of others, too.

- The higher your self-esteem, the more secure, decisive, friendly, trusting, cheerful, optimistic, and purposeful you are. We call this "being empowered."
- The higher your self-esteem, the more able you are to recognize your own worth and achievements without a constant need for approval from others.
- The higher your self-esteem, the more responsibility you take for your own actions.
- The higher your self-esteem, the more willing you are to hang in there, even when the going gets tough. Because you persist, the greater are your chances for experiencing success. Since you have experienced previous successes, you are less likely to be devastated by periodic setbacks.
- The higher your self-esteem, the better able you are to cope with problems because you feel you have the ability to resolve them.

A positive self-esteem is really this important to you and your well-being. How you feel about yourself is obvious to the people around you. Others can tell what you think of yourself because with high self-esteem you project a more confident, assured attitude. This attitude attracts others to you and prompts them to remark, "You really have your act together."

Your sense of self-esteem shows in your appearance, in your actions, in everything you say and do.

TO DO...

1. Describe what self-esteem means to you. Don't use the definition given in this chapter; make one of your own.

_____

_____

_____

_____

_____

_____

_____

_____

_____

2. Describe an incident that you feel helped increase your self-esteem. How did you feel? Can you make it happen again?

_____
_____
_____
_____
_____
_____
_____

3. Describe an incident that decreased your self-esteem. How can you prevent that from happening again?

_____
_____
_____
_____
_____
_____
_____

TO THINK ABOUT...

1. Are you born with high or low self-esteem, or is it developed over time? Is your self-esteem something you can control?

2. How is it possible to have high self-esteem when you must overcome such obstacles as not being smart in school, not being popular, not being good in sports, not dressing like the other kids, and so on?

3. Can't having high self-esteem make you seem conceited and big-headed so that others won't like you? How can you have a healthy sense of self-esteem without going overboard and being obnoxious?

CHAPTER 2

YOU WEAR YOUR SELF-ESTEEM

Your (Self-Esteem) Attitude Is Showing

Because your self-regard is reflected in your behavior, other people can see what you think of yourself. You wear your self-esteem. The way you communicate — your choice of words, how well you listen, your style of relating to (treating) others — are just a few of the many tell-tale signs of how you value yourself.

Another tell-tale sign is who you hang out with — your choice of friends. Have you noticed that people tend to pal around with others who have pretty much the same level of self-esteem as they do? Take a moment and think about your friends. What are their price tags — do they consider themselves valuable merchandise, markdowns, or rejects? In other words, do they have a positive regard for themselves, or not?

Think of yourself as a powerful magnet. There are certain things that you attract. A magnet, because it is metal, attracts metal — like is attracted to like. However, a magnet would not attract wood or water; it attracts things similar to itself. You do too. If you are cheerful and happy and looking for the good side of things, you attract cheerful, happy, positive people. Likewise, if you are negative and gloomy, always whining and complaining, you attract similar people. We are drawn to others whose character and behaviors seem familiar to us.

Some young people are fun and funny and great to be around, while others are depressing, upsetting, or boring to be around. Think about yourself. What do you project to others? If you had to spend the rest of your life in a room with people just like yourself, would you want to? If you wouldn't, you may need to think about making some changes. If life is looking a bit bleak right now, remember that you can choose a new reality — you can change your life. Did you see the movie "Cityslickers?" In one scene a man is complaining that his life is all wrong and he's forever doomed. At that moment a friend looks at him and says, "It doesn't have to be that way forever: In life you get redo's!"

Do you want or need a redo? The good news is that it can be done! But, it's up to you: you get to decide what you want. When it comes to designing what you want out of life, you're in charge. You are the gatekeeper of your life. While you can't always decide on the experiences that come your way, you do get to decide what you will make of those experiences.

Gerry and Miles

Gerry and Miles are tenth graders. Gerry is a big strong football player. He's considered good-looking, but known to have a "chip on his shoulder." Miles, while much smaller, is a good athlete on the track team. Miles has scraggly red hair and a big nose, and all in all, is not visibly good-looking. In fact, he's almost homely.

Although Miles was a good athlete, he used to feel very self-conscious about his looks, so he kept to himself. He had few friends, and he wished he were Gerry. He tried just about everything, including "sucking up" to Gerry. Then one day Miles decided just to forget about being self-conscious over his looks. No matter how much he worried about them, he wasn't going to change the size of his nose, the pigmentation of his skin, or grow five inches. He noticed that when he was always worried about his looks, it seemed he could never make friends or get a date. He decided to look at things differently — basically, to come to his own rescue and be his own best friend. Once Miles stopped comparing himself to Gerry and just enjoyed being himself, his whole life changed. He became happier and friendlier. He didn't seem so uptight and nervous all the time.

His new self-image didn't go unnoticed. When he warmed up to the idea that he was a pretty good guy, others seemed to like him more. His classmates elected him vice-president of his class; his teachers complimented him on his citizenship; he was invited to parties. And then one day, Amanda — who was considered one of the most popular girls in the school — asked him to be her date to homecoming.

Gerry was hoping Amanda would go with him. When she said no, he thought perhaps she would go with Bill or Rex or Allen, the guys who were thought to be the most handsome and popular. "Why on earth did you ask Miles to be your date to homecoming?" Gerry asked her. "I've begged you for months to be my date. And besides, Bill, Rex, or Allen are more your type. They'd do anything to be your date for homecoming. Why Miles? What do you see in that guy?"

"Miles is a happy person, and I think he's fun to be around," replied Amanda. "I like the way he's so sure of himself and the way he thinks about himself. He's friendly and considerate of others. He likes himself, and I like him, too."

As Gerry discovered, it's not just what you look like, or how good you are at sports, or how popular you are that makes you appealing to others: What you think about yourself is also a part of it. In fact, your self-esteem is the first thing people notice about you, and it leaves a more lasting impression than your looks and aptitudes. When you like yourself, people figure you're worth getting to know and so they make an effort to do that.

TO DO . . .

1. Describe your self-esteem.

_____

_____

_____

_____

_____

2. Ask two friends to give you feedback on your self-esteem. Ask: "On a scale of one to ten, in your opinion, what do you think I think about myself?" The goal is to help you see how you wear your self-esteem, to get an idea of how others view what you think about yourself. Note how these scores are alike and/or different. Why do you think that is?

_____

_____

_____

_____

_____

3. List two good friends, two people you barely know, and two people you don't like. Next, rank their self-esteem on a scale of 1 to 10. What do you think their attitude is about themselves? How do those opinions affect your own feelings about them?

Good Friends: **Self-Esteem Rating:**
Name:

_____   _____

_____   _____

What I think they think of themselves:

_____

_____

_____

People I Don't Know Well: **Self-Esteem Rating:**
Name:

_____   _____

_____   _____

What I think they think of themselves:

_____

_____

_____

People I Don't Like Much: **Self-Esteem Rating:**

Name:

_____   _____

_____   _____

What I think they think of themselves:

_____

_____

_____

TO THINK ABOUT...

1. When you have had a bad day, or a terrible experience, is it okay to let your feelings show, or will others think you don't have a high self-esteem and not want to be close to you? Is it important to be upbeat and self-confident all the time?

2. Do you have a friend who is very needy, who always seems to be fishing for compliments and needs you to tell him how wonderful he is? How do you feel about being around someone like that? Do you do that same fishing yourself?

3. Do you show a different you to your parents and family than you do to your friends and classmates? What do your parents think about your level of self-esteem? Do you show a different face in different parts of your life?

CHAPTER 3

"TESTING, TESTING!" How's Your Self-Esteem?

How's Your Self-Esteem?

The nature of your experiences, the events in your life — whether good or bad, positive or negative — contribute to the level of your self-esteem. While you can't always control the events, your response to them is in your control. How you respond affects your self-esteem. How do you think the events of your day add to or detract from your self-esteem?

Self-Esteem Is a Day-by-Day Occurrence

As you read the following statements that describe the events of Amy's day, think about how those events would affect her self-esteem that day. For example, if Amy washed her face and noticed that her complexion was clean and glowing that morning, this would be a plus in her confidence level. If, heaven forbid, she noticed a new pimple on the end of her nose, maybe she would feel self-conscious. Of course, not everything that happens has an effect on self-esteem. If Amy heard on the radio that the school her cousin attends had won a swimming championship, she might not be affected one way or the other, since her cousin was not on the swim team and she had no friends at that school on the winning team.

The purpose of the following exercise is to help you think about how even the little things that happen to you each day can affect your sense of self. Read over the statements, and to the left of each one, rate how you think each event would affect Amy's sense of self that day. Use the number 1 to represent a score of low self-esteem, 10 to represent the highest rating, and 2 to 9 to represent a range of self-esteem.

AMY'S DAY
Self-Esteem Rating

____ a. Amy wakes up to her clock radio playing the song that she and her former boyfriend considered "our song." It's the one that was playing when they met. They broke up last week.

____ b. As Amy brushes her hair, she can't do a thing with it. She is all out of hair spray and mousse. She has a cowlick that she is certain all her friends will tease her about.

____ c. Amy washes her face and notices that her complexion is clean and glowing this morning.

____ d. In school, Amy's best friend tells her that Michael, the most popular boy in the school, said he thought Amy was cute, but dumb.

____ e. Amy tells her friend how "awesome" her new jacket is and how good she looks in it. Her friend says, "Thanks, you always say the nicest things to me! If you ever want to borrow it, it's yours!"

____ f. During lunch, Michael waves at Amy.

____ g. In history class, Amy gets back her paper with a B+ and the comment, "You can do good work when you put your mind to it; maybe the next paper will be an A!"

____ h. Amy gets called on in math class and gives the wrong answer. But she makes a joke out of her mistake, and everyone laughs, including the teacher.

____ i. At volleyball practice after school, Amy gets a note from a best friend saying that she won't be able to go to the school picnic with her this weekend because she and another friend are going out on a double date to the amusement park — with Michael and his friend.

____ j. That night Amy's sister brings home a report with an A+ on it. Late that night Amy hears her mother on the phone with her friend. She brags about the sister's work, but fails to mention that Amy has been selected as one of five "Young Artists" in the city and that her art poster will be displayed downtown in the convention center.

____ k. It's the weekend and Amy has no plans with friends. She feels left out.

____ l. Amy's dog, Bart, senses that Amy is down, so he hops up on her bed and lies next to her, looking sad.

____ m. Amy's father comes in and says he's really proud that she is his daughter; he congratulates her on being selected as an "Outstanding Artist."

____ n. The neighborhood church is having a recycling drive. A next-door neighbor asks Amy to put up posters in the hall announcing the drive.

Here's how Amy ranked these events in terms of their importance to her sense of self. How does this ranking compare to the way you thought these events might affect Amy's perception of herself?

AMY'S RATING

	Low Self-Esteem				No Effect			High Self-Esteem		
	1	2	3	4	5	6	7	8	9	10
Event a	X									
Event b		X								
Event c								X		
Event d		X								
Event e										X
Event f										X
Event g										X
Event h										X
Event i	X									
Event j		X								
Event k		X								
Event l								X		
Event m									X	
Event n					X					

By examining how Amy was affected by certain everday events, you should have a better understanding of how our experiences contribute to or detract from our sense of self. Now it's your turn to see how the events of your days, weeks, and months add to (empower) or take away (erode) your overall self-esteem.

Begin by writing out the events of a day — it could be yesterday or any other particular day. Then, on the grid, rate how each event contributed to your sense of self. How were you affected by these events? I strongly recommend that you do this exercise each day for at least two weeks in a row. Make enough copies of the charting grid on page 23 to do this. This way you will get a chance to see just how the events in your life are contributing overall to high or low self-esteem.

DESCRIPTION OF YOUR DAY

a. _____

b. _____

c. _____

d. _____

e. _____

f. _____

g. _____

h. _____

i. _____

j. _____

	Low Self-Esteem				No Effect			High Self-Esteem		
	1	2	3	4	5	6	7	8	9	10
Event a										
Event b										
Event c										
Event d										
Event e										
Event f										
Event g										
Event h										
Event i										
Event j										

TO DO . . .

1. If you have something that is impossible to change (such as poor eyesight or a physical handicap), how can you "relabel" it to make it something positive? Are there some things that are just so bad they can never be made positive? Is anything ever truly out of your control, or do you get to decide how it will affect your level of self-esteem?

_____
_____
_____
_____

2. What effect do you have on your friends' behavior toward you? Can you "train" your friends to treat you better by rewarding them with certain actions or reactions when they do nice things for you? For example, if you thank your friend for a compliment and compliment him right back, will he be more likely to continue the "compliment circle" and make you feel even better?

_____

_____

_____

_____

3. Is it valid to say that nearly everything has some sort of impact on self-esteem? Can you think of a few things that seem on the surface not to affect you, but can have repercussions on your self-esteem in small ways?

_____

_____

_____

_____

TO THINK ABOUT...

1. Ask a friend to tell you what you did or said that either increased or decreased his or her self-esteem. What did your friend say? Do you do those things intentionally, or do you do them without thinking?

2. Think about several things that happened to you in the past week that did not affect your self-esteem one way or the other. How might you have changed these events a little so that you could have felt better about yourself? For example, when Amy was asked to put up the posters for her friend (an event that had little or no impact on Amy's self-esteem), she could have offered to do even more and been proud of herself for helping someone out when she didn't have to. Or Amy could have used her artistic talents to create an original poster she was proud of.

3. Ask your parents to tell you when you do things that are especially helpful to them. You want to know when you are doing something right so that you can feel good about yourself. Often family members are quick to criticize but slow to praise. Make a family pact to try to praise each other more often, to point out the good things you are doing for each other.

UNIT II

PHYSICAL SAFETY

CHAPTER 4

PHYSICAL SAFETY: Do You Feel Safe at School?

The First Prerequisite: Physical Safety

The passengers have just boarded American Airlines for a flight to New York City. "Welcome aboard flight #1547," says the stewardess. "Your safety is our number one priority." Safety. It assures us that we are in control of our self within our environment, that we have mastery over our being. Physical safety is the first of the six building blocks for developing self-esteem.

Being physically safe means that you can go anywhere without fear of being hurt in any way, or protect yourself by not being in those places that are unsafe. You need to feel safe in your home, in your neighborhood, and most especially in school, where you spend so much of your day. To feel safe requires caring for your body and health as well.

Do You Feel Safe at School?

Think for a moment about how important the feeling of safety is to being able to concentrate on other things. I know that I don't get comfortable in my seat or begin sharing a conversation with a neighboring passenger until the plane is in the air and all feels safe. The airline, too, knows that my feeling safe is important. "Please give us your attention so that we can tell you about the safety rules . . . ," announces the flight attendant.

Just as with the airline industry, physical safety is your school's number one priority and your teacher's primary concern in the classroom. Your safety is your parent's number one concern as well. It's most likely yours, too, even though you may not think about it as such. When you feel physically safe in the classroom and in the school environment — when you needn't worry about being hurt by anyone — you can focus on your schedule of activities and on your role as a learner, and you can enjoy your classmates.

You need to feel safe in the classrooms, in the hallways, on the school grounds. Obviously, the threat of physical harm in the schoolplace is a disturbing experience. When you feel that the school is a safe environment, you are more likely to enjoy your school, teachers, and fellow students. Fear, on the other hand, reduces your ability to concentrate on schoolwork and creates an atmosphere of mistrust. Unfortunately, not all students feel safe at school.

Trinh's Story

Two eighth-grade boys came up to Trinh one day, pushed him into a locker, and demanded he give them his lunch money. They threatened to beat him up unless he agreed to hand over all the money he had that day and one dollar every day from then on. They told him to meet them outside of his English class where he was to give them the money wrapped in a piece of notebook paper. Trinh handed over his money the first time, but when he tried to ignore them the next day, they once again singled him out and threatened him. He began giving them money every day. He was afraid to tell anyone because the older boys told him that if anyone found out, they would come after him.

Darlene's Story

Darlene, a popular cheerleader, demanded that Karen, a bright but timid classmate, do her science homework for her each night. When Karen protested, Darlene said she would spread rumors about Karen if she didn't do what she was asked. Karen was terrified. When she told her best friend, Leann, what Darlene was doing, Leann confronted Darlene. Later in class, Darlene's book "accidentally" slipped and hit Leann in the head as Darlene passed down the aisle on the way to her seat. Darlene was so popular that no one believed Leann when she said Darlene had done it on purpose. Leann got a reputation as someone jealous of Darlene's popularity, and Karen kept on doing the science homework.

Judson's Story

Seventh-grader Judson has been afraid to ride the school bus, ever since the day another student pushed him into Monte. It was an accident and Judson apologized, but Monte punched Judson away, gave him a dirty look, and said, "You'd better never touch me again, you geek!" Now every time Judson boards the bus, Monte and his buddies glare at Judson. He feels nervous and anxious, and is afraid he might get pushed into Monte again. The situation has gotten so bad that Judson is begging his parents to give him a ride to school every day.

Sam's Story

One afternoon Sam innocently walked into the school restroom, interrupting two sixth-grade boys who were smoking. Shoving Sam up against the wall, they threatened to burn him with the cigarette. When he began crying, they made fun of him and shoved him around some more. Although Sam promised not to tell anyone of the incident, the older boys made a point of glaring at him whenever they came across him in the halls or cafeteria. Sam was terrified and for weeks had trouble concentrating.

The many situations in which you can feel unsafe in school or be physically threatened can cause you to feel fear. Although sometimes you might make more of minor situations than they deserve (for example, Judson is probably overly afraid of Monte and exaggerating the problem), nevertheless the fear is very real. When you are afraid, you feel bad, first because you can't defend yourself, and second because you realize others think so little of you that they feel they have a right to dominate you. Both lead to your feeling bad about yourself, or low self-esteem.

FEELING SAFE AT SCHOOL

Are you in a school where you can concentrate on learning rather than on having to deal with real or imaginary dangers? Are you fearful while at school? Many students tell me that the areas in the schoolplace that account for some of their biggest fears include:

- **The restroom:** Students fear encountering other students there who will "rough them up" to make them harbor secrets (from the school staff or other students) about their using drugs or smoking.
- **The bus:** Students fear rowdy, aggressive, and verbally abusive students who force them to leave a favored seat, "just for the fun of it."
- **The empty hallway:** Students fear rowdy, aggressive, and verbally abusive students while they are walking alone.
- **The lunch room:** Students fear being shoved, poked, or pushed out of their place in line, or having lunch money or food stolen.
- **The unsupervised classroom:** Students fear getting into a fight with another student and being hurt or embarrassed in front of other students.

There are also certain types of people that students fear. These include:

- **Bullies:** Every school has some tough guys, or tough girls, who seem to enjoy picking on those who show fear.
- **Foreign students:** Some students are afraid to be around people they can't understand, who speak another language, fearing that these students are talking about and making fun of them.
- **Teachers:** Some teachers project a very stern image, which makes them scary just to look at or think about, even though they may be gentle people once you get to know them.

What You Can Do to Feel Safe at School

Here are some things that you can do to feel safe and be safe in the educational environment. At the end of these suggestions, list other ways you can protect your well-being at school.

1. Know and abide by classroom rules. Posted rules help make it clear to each student that the teacher values the safety of everyone in the room. Be sure you know the rules and why they are in place, then abide by them.

2. Know and abide by school rules. Be aware of the rules and policies that govern school-wide safety. Again, be sure that you know what the rules are and then follow them.

3. Learn about school security. Take the time to learn about security procedures at your school. If rules are lacking or not enforced in your school, talk with the principal and your teacher to discuss what can be done. For example:

- Are the halls, corridors, and grounds well supervised?
- Is the cafeteria supervised?
- Are all school-related functions well supervised?
- Does a patrol car come by to check out the parking lot during evening activities?
- Is the campus well lighted at night?

4. Report students suspected of carrying weapons. If you suspect that a certain student is carrying dangerous objects or weapons, inform your teacher or the principal. You don't have to wait for an incident to occur before measures can be taken to protect you and others.

5. Learn self-management skills. Many young people, when faced with undue harassment by other students, either cannot resolve the problem or are afraid to. If this is happening to you, it may be because you lack certain self-management skills. Assertiveness training, problem-solving, and conflict management are worth learning. I'll be discussing these in later chapters. These skills can greatly add to your sense of personal power and to your ability to protect yourself. There are a number of good books on these topics for young people. The reference section at the back of this book highlights a few, and you may want to ask your school counselor or librarian to suggest others. Additionally, you may want to talk to a teacher to see if the school will offer a mini-course in these areas.

6. Learn more about the people you fear. If you are afraid of a foreign student, seek out someone who knows that person and find out about him or her. You may be pleasantly surprised to know you have a mutual friend or amazed to learn that person is afraid of you too.

7. Try to talk to the people you fear. If you are afraid of a teacher, try to talk to him about something minor, even something like the school's last football game or the local mall that's opening up. What you talk about is not nearly as important as the fact that you begin talking. If you think the teacher is a parent, ask about his or her children. Asking these kinds of questions will show that you care about the teacher as a person, which will make him more open to you and less fearsome.

In short, the more you know, the safer you will feel. The more you know about something, the less power it has over you and the less it can frighten you. You are in control with that knowledge, whether it is of school rules or of the people who seem frightening to you. Think back to how afraid you were the first day at your new school and how silly those fears seem now that you are comfortable. Did you really have to worry about getting lost on campus and being there overnight, alone and forgotten about? Of course not. Once you learned your way around, those fears evaporated. The same can be true of most fears for your physical safety once you learn how many precautions there are and how much your school truly cares about keeping you safe.

TO DO...

1. Describe your school in terms of safety. Do you know where the fire exits are? Do you know where the fire extinguishers are and how to use them? Do you have fire drills? Do you feel the school building is strong and able to withstand storms or earthquakes or tornadoes? Is there anything about your school campus that frightens you physically?

_____

_____

_____

_____

2. Describe any fears you may have about the people on your campus. Are there bullies who bother you? Are there gangs or cliques that you want to avoid? How do you act around these people? How does being afraid of them make you feel?

_____

_____

_____

_____

3. Go back through exercises one and two. For every fear you have, write down a suggestion on how to deal with and overcome it. For example, if you are concerned that the school is in a bad neighborhood, talk to the principal about the safety measures she has instigated. Learn about the guards and the police patrols. Talk to your friends and see how they feel. Are they just as or more frightened than you are? Talk with a teacher (or your parents) about your fears, or to express concern about a friend who is feeling fearful. The more information you have, the safer you will feel.

Fear:_____

How it can be resolved:_____

_____

Fear:_____

How it can be resolved:_____

_____

4. List the safety rules currently displayed and enforced in your room and explain why these rules are important.

Rule:_____

Why it's important: _____

_____

Rule:_____

Why it's important: _____

_____

5. Think about the safety measures designed for your school. What other rules need to be put in place?

_____

_____

_____

_____

6. Think about the safety rules currently displayed and enforced on the school grounds. What else needs to be done?

_____

_____

_____

_____

TO THINK ABOUT...

1. Is physical safety something you usually think about? Is it important for students to know how safe the school is, or is that something you take for granted?

2. Is it good to talk about your fears, or do you think your friends will think you are silly if you bring them up? If you are afraid, whom can you talk to about your fears?

3. Is there anything you can do to improve safety, or is that out of your control? If you think the school is unsafe physically, or if you are afraid to walk down the halls, how can you change matters?

CHAPTER 5

PHYSICAL SAFETY: Do You Feel Safe at Home and in Your Neighborhood?

Safety in Your Home and Neighborhood

Another important source of your sense of safety comes from how safe you feel in your home and neighborhood. You may live in a dangerous neighborhood, or perhaps one or both parents or other adults at home are hurting you physically. Coming from a frightening neighborhood or an unsafe home can cause you to be hurt, and create emotional turmoil; you feel as though you are powerless, incapable of being in charge of what is happening to you. Worrying about your physical safety blocks you from moving beyond fear and experiencing the joy and well-being that you deserve. Spending your days in fear and anxiety can be very draining.

Or perhaps you have nothing to worry about. When you feel safe, you are more confident in the sense of being in control of your life.

What's Your Home Life Like?

The safety and comfort of your home is the foundation of your life. No matter how many hours you spend at school or with friends, you always come back home. Your home should be a safe haven, a refuge, a welcoming place where you can be secure. But what happens when home is one of your problems?

Jessica's Story

Jessica is a senior in high school. Her parents don't bother to hide their arguments anymore. They figure that "Jessie's old enough to know the way things are." A few times her parents got into a physical fight, throwing shoes and hitting each other. Jessica is too embarrassed to talk about her fears with her friends or the counselor at school, so she holds them in. She worries that her parents will seriously hurt each other, or that one of them will go to jail, since each constantly threatens the other with calling the police. Having read and seen television shows on spouse abuse, she is scared that one or both of her parents may go too far and seriously hurt the other. Jessica is also afraid that she might get hit or hurt if she gets in the middle of the fight; therefore she tries to avoid going home as much as possible. She is not only ashamed of her parents but ashamed of herself for being afraid of them. She thinks she must be a "bad daughter" for not wanting to be with her parents and wishes she could be more like her best friend Karen who seems to get along great with her family.

What is your home life like for you? It's different for all of us, so what seems like chaos to one may not be to another. What's important is that it feels safe for you to be there. How would you rate your home in terms of safety? Ask yourself these questions:

- How safe is my home? Explain.

___

- Are there places in my home that are frightening to me?

___

- How much time do I spend at home alone?

___

- In case of an emergency, do I know what to do, whom to call, and where to go?

___

- Do I look forward to coming home? Am I eager to spend time at home, or would I rather stay away as much as possible?

___

- Do I view all family members (and anyone else living there) as nonthreatening people? Am I comfortable staying home alone with my brothers, sisters, stepparents?

___

- Am I proud to bring friends home, to show off my home and especially my room?

___

- Do I feel that this is "my home," not just "my parents' home?"

___

■ What is my parents' philosophy of discipline? Is it fair or harsh?

_____

_____

Sexual Abuse

Being sexually victimized takes an enormous toll on the value a person places on her self-worth. A victim of sexual abuse suffers physical hurt and emotional pain that can last a lifetime; as a result, the victim may hurt others later in life.

If you are a victim of sexual abuse, report it. Your teachers, counselors, principal, and school nurse are specifically trained to know whom to contact to help you, and how to protect you and your identity. Ask these adults where to go to seek help, or to get help for someone you know (or suspect) is being sexually abused.

SAFETY IN YOUR NEIGHBORHOOD

It used to be that young people always attended schools in their own neighborhoods. Today, however, many students are bused to other schools. Perhaps, like Gwen, you are an outsider in your own neighborhood.

Gwen's Story

Gwen moved to her neighborhood last year from out of state. Coming at the end of summer, she didn't have much time to make friends. She was looking forward to getting to know people in school. However, she was bused to a school several miles away, the only one from her neighborhood to go there. When she got home, the other kids all made fun of her for going to a "posh" school and accused her of thinking she was better than they were. They made her feel like she didn't belong and never invited her to do anything with them. She had friends at her school, but they lived so far away that Gwen rarely saw them after school. She began to fear getting on and off the bus, knowing that if anyone in the neighborhood saw her she would be picked on.

Maybe your problem is different. Maybe you're like Aaron.

Aaron's Story

Aaron grew up in his neighborhood and knows everyone who lives there. He experiences a lot of pressures to hang out with the guys, to do the things they do. Aaron is on the swim team at school, and likes to hang out with his friends from there. This makes the neighborhood boys jealous and angry. They taunt Aaron about dumping his friends and shove him around. It has gotten to the point where Aaron is afraid to bring his swim team friends home, and he avoids his neighborhood friends as much as possible.

Not everyone feels safe in his neighborhood. Do you? Answering the following questions can help you identify whether you feel safe and comfortable, or whether fear of your physical environment is causing you problems.

■ Do I live in a safe neighborhood? Explain.

_____
_____

■ Are there neighbors I feel comfortable asking for help if I need it?

_____
_____

■ Describe a "safe" neighborhood.

_____
_____

TO DO...

1. Make a list of the sources of "physical" fears.

_____
_____

2. Think of a time when fear (of home or family) made you act differently than you otherwise would have. Describe that situation. Then describe how you felt about your actions as well as how the people around you felt.

_____
_____

TO THINK ABOUT...

1. How can you tell whether your fears about your home are justified or not? Whom can you talk with about them that you can trust not to make fun of you or tell anyone else?

2. How much control does a young person have over his or her home life? For example, if a father hits a mother, what should you do?

3. How can you not let fear rule your life? If you are truly physically frightened of a situation that you probably can't change and that won't change itself (like living in a neighborhood with gangs), how can you feel good about yourself when you are afraid? When is it all right to be afraid?

CHAPTER 6

PHYSICAL SAFETY: Who's in Charge —You or Drugs?

Be Powerful Enough to Just Say No!

Growing up today isn't easy. You have to face pressures from your teachers, your parents, your coaches, your peers, and many others. All this pressure can lead to stress, which makes you feel hyper, or tired and sluggish, or incapable of doing anything. Those are terrible feelings. Some kids will do anything to feel better, including taking drugs or drinking. They like the momentary high they get, and they reassure themselves by saying, "Oh, I can handle this. It's just one joint, or just one drink. Everyone does it. I won't let it get out of hand." Yet, using drugs or drinking is not a shortcut to growing up. All it does is shortchange you by ruining your health, by getting you into trouble with your parents, teachers, and maybe even the law, and by making you ashamed of yourself for letting drugs or alcohol, not you, be in charge.

"Lucky" Jay

When Jay was in eighth grade, his friends called him "Lucky" Jay. He seemed to have everything. He had great parents who were "cool" and let him have a late curfew. He excelled in sports, made good grades, and had the kind of good looks that made him popular with the girls. Friends always teased him about having a perfect life, saying they wished they could be like him. But as Jay tells it, he didn't feel so lucky himself.

"I felt like I was seeing a stranger every time I looked in the mirror. That guy, the one the girls thought was cute, I thought was ugly. Whenever I'd get an A in class, instead of enjoying it, all I could think about was how much work I'd have to do to get an A the next time. I hated going to soccer workouts because I knew the other guys were all trying to show the coach they were better than me. The pressure was just too much. I started drinking, getting an older guy to buy me a six pack at the 7-11 store.

"I really liked the feeling alcohol gave me. It sort of made me forget all my worries, made me feel that nothing was worth getting upset about. I bragged to my friends about my drinking and liked the way they treated me — like a big man. Then a senior offered me some pot. I couldn't turn it down and still seem cool to my friends, so I smoked it. And then some more, and more, and more. Soon I was smoking pot every day. Everything changed.

"I just didn't care about anything. I didn't care about soccer and didn't work hard at practices, which made the coach bench me. I didn't care about grades, and went from A's and B's to C's and D's. You talk about my parents getting upset! My dad actually went hoarse from shouting at me so much. I shouted back once and got grounded for two weeks. But I didn't care; I sat in my room and smoked some more dope. It was a vicious cycle. I did drugs to feel better about myself, but I'd end up feeling worse, so I'd do more drugs. Getting high was no longer something I did to feel happy and have fun; it was something I had to do just to feel 'normal.' I wasn't in control anymore.

"The final straw came when I needed money for my pot and I shoplifted something from a store. The manager called the police who took me to jail. My parents came to get me and everything was pretty wild for a while. But you know, that turned out to be the best thing that ever happened to me. I felt relieved that I had been caught. I could be up front with my folks now and get some help. Today, a year later, I'm sober; I don't have to do drugs to feel good about myself. For the first time, I do feel like I deserve to be called Lucky Jay."

Free From Drugs and Alcohol

Like Jay, many people think they can cope with pressures by having just one drink, just one joint. They have a low self-esteem and need to bolster it by looking like a big man in front of their friends. They mistakenly think that getting drunk gives them that image. How can you avoid falling into the same trap that Jay fell into? How can you cope with your life and avoid drugs, especially when everyone around you seems to be doing them and thinks they're okay or "cool" to do? Here are a few suggestions:

1. Have the courage to say no. Like most kids, you'll probably be offered your first drink or drugs by someone at school. Learn to say no quickly, loudly, and firmly. Make your opinion known immediately. If you hesitate, the person offering you the drugs will keep on insisting. If you say, "No way!" and make the other person feel ridiculous for even offering, you win his respect and keep your own self-respect.

2. Role-play saying no without an excuse or justification or long explanation. Someone offering you pot doesn't have to hear a lecture on why you don't touch the stuff. Practice with a friend. Pretend you're in the school hallways, at a game, at the mall. Rehearse saying no without any more explanation. Practice laughing it off or just walking away if someone makes fun of you for being a "goody two shoes."

3. Don't drink. Here are some ideas to help you and your friends:

- Fill your glass with 7-Up or Coke to discourage anyone from trying to give you a drink.
- Announce ahead of time that you are not going to drink. Be aware that this may result in added peer pressure, however, people should respect you for being up front.
- Volunteer to be the designated driver.

"But It's Only a Cigarette!"

After all this talk about alcohol and drugs, cigarettes may seem pretty tame. A lot of young people say, "Hey, my parents should be happy I'm smoking. After all, it's not like

I'm doing drugs or drinking. It's just a cigarette!" But tobacco is a drug, too, and can be just as deadly and costly as other drugs. As you probably know already, there is a lot of peer pressure to smoke. Even the "straight" kids can be smokers. How can you avoid picking up the habit?

1. Look at heavy smokers. Notice how their breath stinks? Their whole body has a stale odor that is disgusting. Now think of whether that cute boy or girl you have your eye on would want to be around that. Remember, even your best friends won't tell you to your face that you stink, but they sure will talk about it behind your back.

2. Keep a list of items you want to buy. If you saved $2 a day (the cost of just one pack of cigarettes), how quickly could you buy them? In one year you would spend $730 on cigarettes. For that kind of money you could fly to Europe, buy a new bike, or go on a great shopping spree. Why let your money go up in smoke?

3. Watch someone who is a heavy smoker gasp for breath. Ever hear of emphysema? That's a lung disease in which people can't seem to get enough air into their lungs. They gasp and wheeze and choke as if they are suffocating. How would you like to go through all that? Read up on the various diseases you can get from smoking: lung cancer, heart disease, and many others.

4. Try not to be around smokers. This is difficult if your peer group has smokers in it, but it's important. When everyone around you smokes, you begin to feel that it's no big deal. You don't notice the yellow teeth and the awful smell so much. It's easier to begin when everyone else is puffing away. It's much simpler to say no when no one else is smoking.

TO DO . . .

1. Is it possible to stay in control while drinking just a little or smoking pot just a little? How can you tell when drugs or alcohol begins to control someone's life?

_____
_____
_____
_____
_____

2. If your friends are pressuring you to do drugs, whom can you talk to about the problem? Is your teacher the best one, or should you talk to your parents? How can you ask for your parents' help without them making you stop hanging around with people

who do drugs? Can you be friends with people who smoke or drink if you don't smoke or drink yourself?

3. What does taking drugs do to your self-esteem? Think of people you know who do drugs or drink. How do they feel about themselves? How do you think they'll turn out in ten or twenty years? What will they be like as adults?

TO THINK ABOUT...

1. Make a list of the ways people act when they are drunk. For example, they bellow, scream, cry, drool, and spit; they throw up all over their friends. Think of all the ways you have seen people make fools of themselves when they are high. Then think about whether you want your friends, your girlfriend or boyfriend, or your parents to see you like that.

2. Read biographies or articles on famous people who used drugs or alcohol but gave them up. Study how they often had to get very sick or nearly ruin their lives before they found the strength to change. Read how they all say they wish they had never started. Make a list of people (such as famous rock stars, artists, writers) whose lives were cut short by drug overdoses.

3. Put together a small skit in which people say no to drugs and drinking, making it funny and personal to your school. Ask your teacher if you can present it in class. Your goal is to get everyone thinking about drugs and how stupid it is to use them. Help your friends see that it's cooler not to do drugs.

CHAPTER 7

PHYSICAL SAFETY: Are You Taking Care of Your Body?

You Count on Your Body (for Life)

Would you go into a building if it were dilapidated and might fall down on you any minute? Would you feel comfortable in a schoolroom that smelled funny and creaked a lot? Of course not. You wouldn't feel safe if the building you're in weren't strong and secure.

Think of your body as the building around you. It, too, has to be strong and secure, in good shape, in order for you to be physically safe. Just as you have to count on the school building not to tumble down around your head when there's a strain on it (such as a heavy thunderstorm), so you need to be able to count on your body to help you get through the physical demands of life.

When the bell rings and you are going to be late for class, you count on your legs to get you down the hall in a hurry. When your best friend is talking to that cute new boy in the lunchroom, you count on your hearing to let you eavesdrop just enough to hear the good stuff. Every day you take your body for granted, assuming that it is going to be healthy and sound. But how safe is that dependence? Be good to your body: Life is a wonderful adventure and you want your body to help you experience it to the fullest.

Kimberly and Denise

Kimberly and Denise are best friends in the sixth grade. Denise has a sweet tooth and is always eating chocolates. She gets a lot of toothaches that she doesn't tell her parents about because she knows they will make her go to the dentist. Whenever she has a toothache, she gets grumpy and snaps at Kimberly. Last week the two friends had a big fight. Denise tried to apologize.

"I'm sorry I yelled at you. You know I didn't mean it. You know that's just the way I am."

Kimberly shook her head. "You shouldn't eat so much candy. You know what it does to you. It makes you grumpy. And you never want to do anything fun since you gained weight. You never want to ride bikes or go roller blading or even take a walk. You're just no fun to be around."

Denise was almost in tears. "It's not my fault. You can't blame me."

"I do blame you!" said Kimberly. "You're not a baby. You took Ms. Buchanan's health class. You know how to eat right and get exercise. If you don't eat right, you always feel lousy."

HOW TO IMPROVE YOUR HEALTH

Setting Lifelong Patterns in Your Diet

No matter how young you are you need to eat right. Some scientists say that the way we eat as children determines our health for the rest of our lives. Certainly, if you don't eat right, you won't grow strong. The eating habits you develop now will set the pattern for later. If you want to be the best you can be, if you want to feel that you are safe in your body, take the time to learn about nutrition and follow some basic rules.

1. Always eat breakfast. You may still be sleepy in the morning and feel you can't face food, but breakfast is the most important meal of the day. It is the fuel that starts your body's engine. If you are responsible for making your own breakfast, it might be easier to handle if you prepare some of it the night before. Set the breakfast table. Put out the bowl, utensils, cereal box, glasses. All you'll have to do in the morning is pour the cereal and milk and maybe fix a piece of toast. Breakfast doesn't have to be huge, just nourishing.

2. Try to eat a balanced diet. A balanced diet does not mean a candy bar in one hand and potato chips in the other. It means that you have some fruit, vegetables, meat, pasta (like spaghetti), bread, cereal, and dairy products regularly. Of course, you don't eat everything at one sitting! Ask your parents if you can help plan your own meals. Make sure you eat a variety of healthful foods. You can also have the occasional candy bar, as long as it's after you've eaten properly.

3. Be careful of diets. You may think you are overweight and decide to skip eating for a while. That's one of the worst things you can do. Not eating can give you headaches, and dizziness, and cause you to become short-tempered and grumpy. Plus, you will probably get so hungry that you break the diet and eat more than you would have originally. If you need to lose weight, ask your parents for help. Lose a little at a time, in a way that's safe.

4. Don't use food as a crutch. Sometimes young people who are depressed use food to make themselves feel better. Doesn't that sound just like what you learned in the previous chapter about people who use drugs to feel better? Of course, there's no comparison between a Snickers and a marijuana cigarette, but food can control you just as much as drugs.

Exercise Can Give You Energy

When someone asks you to exercise, do you ever say, "I can't; I just don't have the energy!" Did you know that exercising can actually make you feel more energetic? Not only does exercise strengthen muscles, but it increases blood circulation, adds oxygen to the body, and relaxes the nerves.

When you take a brisk walk, or go for a swim, or skate, you come back refreshed. You recharge your batteries. You may feel tired, but it's a good tiredness. The more you exercise, the stronger your body becomes and the better you feel. Here are some suggestions:

1. Set up a regular exercise program. For exercise to do its job, it must be regular. Develop a routine. Make exercising as much a part of your day as brushing your teeth and washing your face.

2. Make exercise fun. You don't have to lie on your bedroom floor counting out sit-ups and tummy crunches. There are many things you can do for exercise. Choose what is fun for you. You don't have to do the same activities everyone else is doing; come up with what works best for you. This is important because if exercise isn't fun, you won't keep it up.

3. Work out with friends. It's more fun to work out when you have someone to talk to. Plus, you can encourage each other. You can make sure each of you works out on those days when you're just not in the mood. Since people are so busy these days, working out together can be one way of spending time with friends you might not get to see much of otherwise.

4. Set goals. Write up a contract, sign it and have someone witness it (it's harder to cheat this way!). You might say, for instance, that by the first of next month you'll be swimming 10 laps, then 20 the following month, and so on. You're less likely to get bored by exercise if you have a definite goal and can see your progress.

5. Reward yourself! When you've had a good workout or met a goal, give yourself a prize. It may be a new tee shirt, a cassette, or just a night at the movies. Make it something that you've been wanting to do. Your parents will probably be so proud of you for meeting your goal they'll be glad to help.

6. Don't overdo it. Beginners get so excited about exercise that they go overboard and then get so sore that they quit the next day. Take a break. Develop a routine that allows you to work out progressively harder, but program in time for rest and relaxation as well. Learn to slow down and relax at the end of the routine.

Remember, your body is the building you live in every day. In order to feel safe, you need to have that building in tip-top shape. That means taking care of yourself through proper diet and exercise. You are the one who's in control, so why not be as strong and healthy as possible?

TO DO . . .

1. For the next few weeks, keep a log of what you eat and how much you exercise. Notice when you feel particularly energetic or sluggish, and look at what you ate that day. Are there certain meals that make you feel peppy, other foods that make you feel sluggish or slow you down? When you exercise, how do you feel?

_____

_____

_____

_____

2. How can you exercise if you have no time, if you've already got a full schedule? What can you do if there are no exercise facilities around you, such as a swimming pool or a gym? What types of exercises are easy to do anywhere and don't take a lot of time?

_____

_____

_____

_____

_____

3. When you go to a restaurant, what healthful foods can you choose? Can you eat out, say at a McDonald's, and still choose nutritious foods?

_____

_____

_____

_____

_____

TO THINK ABOUT...

1. If your parents are in charge of buying groceries and cooking meals, how can you get them to give you more nutritious food? Can you make suggestions or go shopping with them? If your parents both work and have little time for preparing meals, can you help out?

2. Make a pledge with your family to improve your health. Draw up a formal diet and exercise plan created by everyone jointly. Involve each member of your family, even the very young children. Give prizes for the members who stick most closely to the plan. Think of a special, fun, family outing as a reward.

3. Observe the kids in your school. Watch what they eat in the cafeteria. How do the meals of the kids who are upbeat, energetic, and fun differ from those who are grumpy and slow? Can you find similar patterns in their exercise?

UNIT III

EMOTIONAL SECURITY

CHAPTER 8

EMOTIONAL SECURITY: What Tune (Message) Is Playing in Your Head?

What Are You Telling Yourself?

A second aspect of self-esteem is feeling emotionally secure — for example, when you aren't fearful of being made to feel unworthy, or when you feel safe from intimidations or put-downs. It's demeaning to have someone swear at you, make you feel unimportant, say something unkind or sarcastic, or not show respect or pay attention when you're talking. These "put-downs" tear down. They hurt and can have long-term effects, especially if you believe them.

The actions and words of others can shape your "inner language," that is, what you tell yourself about your self-worth. That can be good or bad depending on whether they said something positive or negative. Just as positive statements are self-esteem building, negative statements are detrimental to self-esteem.

Our inner language has a powerful effect on us. It creates our reality. Self-statements such as "I can't," "I'm fat," "I'm ugly," or "I'm dumb" obviously do little to promote a positive sense of self. When you make statements such as "I can do it," "I'm okay," or "I'm capable," you send yourself messages that add to a positive sense of self.

Ricardo's Story

Ricardo was the youngest of four children. When he was seven, his father died of cancer. His mother, who had left school in the eleventh grade to raise a family, worked hard to support herself and her four children. "Even though our lives seem shattered," she told them when their father died, "we will stay together and be a happy family. We will survive intact. I don't yet know how we will do that, but we can, and we will."

As impossible as the odds seemed, all four children not only graduated from high school but went on to college. Two graduated with advanced degrees. Ricardo graduated at the top of his class. Today he is happily married, the father of two children, and a successful businessman. "To tell the truth," he said, "I don't know how my mother did it, but she did. My mother convinced us kids that we were going to persevere, and we did. Although we grew up without money, and I for one differentiate not having money from being poor, we always knew that we were going to make it. There were times when I thought about giving up but that inner voice always said, 'You can, and you will.'"

Whitney's Story

Whitney overheard two girls in the bathroom talking about her one day. "I wish I were as smart as Whitney. She always knows the right answer. Sometimes I think she knows the question before the teacher even asks it!" The other girl nodded. "It's not fair. Brains and beauty too." Whitney stood there surprised to learn what the other girls thought about her. The rest of the day she was just glowing. "They think I'm smart and pretty! They want to be like me! I can't believe it!" Whitney had always thought of herself as just okay, as average, nothing special. That one conversation led her to acquiring a cheerfulness and confidence that showed, and it made her respect herself so much more. As she played their conversation over and over again in her mind, she began to believe it; this belief in herself gave her strength, leading to increased self-esteem, leading to even more confidence. She had begun a cycle that could only make her feel better and happier.

Are You a Sissy or a Ferrari?

That we become what we believe can be good news — if what we believe is esteem building. Think back to the story in Chapter One of the young boy who came home crying because a classmate had called him a sissy. How about you? What do you believe about yourself? Ask yourself the following questions and write down your answers.

1. Did your parents lead you to believe you were a sissy or a Ferrari?

   _____

   _____

2. What did they *say* that led you to this conclusion?

   _____

   _____

3. What did they *do* that led you to this conclusion?

   _____

   _____

4. Did a particular teacher lead you to believe you were a sissy or a Ferrari?

   _____

   _____

5. What did he or she *say* that led you to this conclusion?

   _____

   _____

6. What did he or she *do* that led you to this conclusion?

   _____

   _____

7. Did your best friend lead you to believe you were a sissy or a Ferrari?

   _____

   _____

8. What did he or she *say* that led you to this conclusion?

   _____

   _____

9. What did he or she *do* that led you to this conclusion?

   _____

   _____

10. Whom do you think has the most influence on your perception of yourself? Is this good (builds your self-esteem) or bad (erodes your self-esteem)?

    _____

    _____

11. What can you do if you want to change the influence someone has on you?

    _____

    _____

12. If you're a sissy but you'd rather be a Ferrari, what can you do?

    _____

    _____

Empowering Your Inner Language

Like the boy who felt bad because he had been told he was a sissy and believed it, but later realized he could decide what he was, you can change negative (dysfunctional) self-statements. You can program yourself just like a computer. You can develop an inner language that is positive and supportive, one that builds your self-esteem. Here are the steps:

1. Use positive language. The first step is to be aware of the kind of language you use. Is it positive, supportive, and encouraging? What is the nature of the language you use with friends, teachers, parents? Do you encourage them and build their self-esteem? Aside from what you are telling them, what are you telling *you* about you? Are you more likely to say, "You can do it!" or "Oh, I'm so stupid?"

2. Label the language. Use terms to label your language. Call the positive statements "fuzzies" or "compliments." Label negative comments "zingers" or "put-downs."

3. Insist on positive language. Don't talk negatively about yourself or others and request the same from them. Many times your friends or family members have used put-down statements so often that they've actually conditioned themselves to say the negative without realizing what they are saying. Gently correct them. When you hear a negative statement, tell the other person, "You just made a zinger, putting me down! Did you know you were putting me down?" Calling the put-down to the other person's attention will probably result in his being more conscious of his cruelty and taking steps to stop it. On the other hand, it is important to call attention to the positive statements as well. When someone says something nice about you, tell him, "That was a really nice thing to say to me; I felt so good when you said that!" Chances are, you will make him feel good about himself at the same time, and he will want to give you even more compliments.

4. Compliment others. Statements like, "I appreciate it when you . . ." "I feel good about myself when I . . ." "I really like it when you . . ." "Thank you," "Thanks," "Thanks for noticing," or "When you help me I feel . . ." are all statements of common courtesy. Get in the habit of using them.

What to Do About Negative Self-Talk

Habits are easy to make but hard to break. With most habits, we don't even know what we are doing because we do them automatically. If you speak badly about yourself, you need to recognize that habit and stop it immediately before it becomes even more ingrained. When you recognize your negative thinking patterns, you can change them, as the following examples show.

Paul's Story

Paul barges his way to the head of the lunch line. Mr. Hanson notices and calls him on it. "I know you're eager to have lunch, Paul, but you must wait your turn in line like everyone else." Paul begins to process this message. Here are two possible scenarios of his thinking.

Paul's Thoughts: "Mr. Hanson is mad at me. If he liked me, he wouldn't embarrass me in front of the other kids."
Paul's Feelings: Upset, angry, defensive.
Paul's Behavior: He stomps out of line and leaves the lunch room, muttering under his breath how unfair Mr. Hanson is.

Here Paul assumes that it's Mr. Hanson who has made him upset and angry and that he therefore has a right to be defensive. After all Mr. Hanson did reprimand him. In this case, what Paul is thinking is irrational and affects his behavior in a negative way. A different and more positive scenario on Paul's part might be as follows.

Paul's Thoughts: "I wish I had stayed in line. I know the rule, and it doesn't feel good to be reminded of it in front of the other students."
Paul's Feelings: Rational, feeling responsible.
Paul's Behavior: "I'm sorry Mr. Hanson. I know I'm supposed to wait in line."

As this example shows, it's not so much the event that determines your behavior as how you think about it.

Changing Unwanted Thoughts

When Suzanne receives a low grade on her first math test, she tells herself that she is dumb and not capable of doing the work. She believes that failing this one math test means that she will fail all the others, so she skips math class on the day of her next test. Suzanne's coping style is affected negatively by what she has told herself about her abilities.

Beliefs that work against you place limits on what you will attempt to do. For example, Suzanne's beliefs about her potential to do math are dysfunctional. In contrast, beliefs that enhance or improve your coping ability work for you. You must be able to distinguish between the situation itself and what you say to yourself about it. It doesn't make sense that Suzanne should skip math class simply because she failed one exam. Unwanted or irrational thoughts can be changed to positive ones. The first step is thought-stopping.

Thought-Stopping

Once you're aware of how inner thoughts work for or against you, you'll want to be able to change the negative thoughts. This procedure is called *thought-stopping*. To begin, visualize a stop sign whenever you start telling yourself limiting statements. This stop sign acts as a signal to stop thinking dysfunctional thoughts. In the previous example, Suzanne told herself that because she failed a math test she would fail again; therefore, she skipped class to avoid repeating an unpleasant situation. The last phase of thought-stopping involves thought substitution. Here Suzanne would visualize a stop sign, and then generate as many positive thoughts as possible, such as:

"Just because I failed one test doesn't mean I'll fail all other math tests."
"Failing a test doesn't mean I'm dumb."
"I should study harder next time."
"I could attend review sessions and ask for extra help if I feel I need it."

You can reshape negative messages by focusing on the things you do well. The goal is to think about the approach you bring to schoolwork, relationships, and life.

Rewriting Negative Messages

Another way you can turn negative thoughts into positive ones is by clarifying what is really going on. Separate what is true from what isn't; in other words, rewrite these messages. For example:

Example: School is hard for me.
Rewrite: I enjoy all my subjects except algebra. I did well in math class, but I don't yet understand all the concepts of algebra. I need more help in that class.

Example: I am unpopular.
Rewrite: I'd like to be friends with Karen and Debra, but I'm not certain they want my friendship.

If you think that you're not a good student, you will probably find school difficult, and this will contribute to your not liking school. Likewise, if you seek someone's friendship but don't get it, you may feel unpopular. Changing or rewriting the way you think about yourself is important because when you send mostly positive messages to yourself, you are more likely to have the courage to go forward when things get tough. When you do well, you start that wonderfully contagious success cycle that enables you to excel in your day-to-day work, in your relationships with others, and best of all, to enjoy positive feelings that contribute to your growing sense of self-worth.

TO DO . . .

1. Have a round-table class discussion of name-calling. How does it feel to be called names? What can you say in return to discourage another student who insists on being negative? Talk about the good-neutral-bad ways to make a point. Examples:

   Negative: Geez, when was the last time you brushed your teeth, Christmas?

   Positive: My mom gave me a package of Lifesaver Breath Mints. I'm eating one, would you like one?

   Negative: You never shut up. Do you have to comment on everything all the time?

   Positive: I like how you are open and willing to communicate. People learn a lot by listening to you, but maybe you could listen to other people sometimes and learn from them, too.

2. Discuss a time when your feelings were hurt by your parents' name-calling. What can you do to help your parents understand the benefits of positive and encouraging language?

_____
_____
_____
_____
_____

3. Think about the comments you have heard people say about others. Pretend they are directed at you. How does each one make you feel? What does each one do to your self-esteem? For example, if you heard, "Gina needs to work harder; she could be an A student if she tried," does that depress you or motivate you? How do you respond to praise and criticism?

_____
_____
_____
_____
_____

TO THINK ABOUT...

1. Which is more important, emotional or physical security? Are the two interconnected? Can you have one without the other?

2. Are people who brag a lot and talk constantly about themselves secure or insecure emotionally? How can you tell? Can you be secure about some areas of your life and insecure about others? Is it possible to increase your security with a plan, or is your security determined by forces outside of your control?

3. Can others make you feel secure or insecure, or do you do that to yourself? While others can control your physical surroundings, can they control your mind? Can you change your mind to make yourself happier? How can you program your inner tape with positive language?

CHAPTER 9

EMOTIONAL SECURITY: What Do You Get Stressed Out About?

Understanding Fears and Anxieties

Have you ever thought that you were not as attractive, not as intelligent, not as popular as others? Sometimes the worries are justified, sometimes not. You can worry yourself to the point where you believe the worst about yourself, or you can work toward understanding your fears and anxieties, and overcome them.

Everyone has concerns, from the young child who is worried that Mom will never come back if she so much as leaves the room, to the eighteen-year-old who feels that if he doesn't get a job or acceptance into a good college, his future is doomed. Insecurities are a natural part of life; everyone has them, so you are not abnormal for being afraid or stressed out. By using stress as a motivator, by turning a disadvantage into an advantage, you enhance your self-esteem.

George's Story

George wrote an essay on Citizenship that won a district-wide award, and now he has to give a speech in front of his classmates at school. While George is proud of his writing and likes to write, he is afraid to talk in front of people. To make matters worse, he has braces; he thinks he lisps and even spits sometimes when he talks. He tries to get out of doing the speech, but the teacher insists. George is going to be part of an assembly, speaking right after one of the most popular students in the school. Certain that he will look bad by comparison, he is so concerned that he can't sleep the night before.

George's dad talks to him that morning, telling him that it is natural to be worried, but that he should use that nervous energy to recharge himself. He takes him through an exercise wherein George sees himself giving the speech, pausing for a laugh at the right place, getting a lot of applause at the end. When George gets through the speech, he sees his friends stomping and whistling, and feels pretty good about himself. As he tells his best friend Suzie, "I wanted my mom to call the school and tell them I was sick this morning, but I forced myself to go to school. Now I'm glad I did, because if I can do this, I can do anything!"

By imagining himself confronting his fear, George became a stronger, more confident person.

YOU CAN LEARN TO MANAGE YOUR STRESS

What Is Stress?

Most people think of stress as the daily demands of life. Technically, these demands are called stressors. Stress is the actual wear and tear on our body. Whether the stressor is a biochemical insult (for example, a dose of drugs or alcohol), physical injury, or emotional arousal (fear, anger, love), the mind and body respond in the same manner. Stress has three stages: (1) alarm reaction, (2) resistance, and (3) exhaustion.

Alarm Reaction. You may recognize some of the following alarm reaction responses from your own experience.

1. Have you ever had "knots" or "butterflies" (or "eagles"!) in your stomach before taking an exam or making a presentation in front of others? Because it is more important to be alert and strong in the face of danger than to digest food, your digestion slows so blood may be directed to your muscles and brain.

2. Can you remember trying to catch your breath after being frightened (like the time you were at your desk concentrating on an exam when a breeze caused the door to slam shut)? This reaction is due to breathing faster to supply more oxygen for the needed muscles.

3. Do you remember how your heart pounded when that speeding car wheeled around the corner and just missed you? In such situations the heart speeds up and blood pressure soars, forcing blood to parts of your body that need it.

4. Have you noticed that you use extra deodorant when you know you are going to be under stress, like making an important presentation before others, or asking someone special for a date when you are unsure whether that person will accept? Perspiration increases to cool the body.

5. Do you ever have a stiff neck or chest pain after a stressful day? This occurs because muscles tense in preparation for important action.

6. Have you noticed how quickly some wounds stop bleeding? Chemicals are released to make the blood clot more rapidly. If you are injured, this clotting can reduce blood loss.

7. Remember getting your "second wind" the time your best friend was involved in a confrontation and you rushed over to help? Or were you once surprised by your strength and endurance during an emergency, for instance, when you could tell from your dog's yelp that he needed help? The extra strength came from sugars and fats pouring into your bloodstream to provide fuel for quick energy.

Resistance Stage. Almost immediately following a stressful event the body attempts to return to its normal balance (homeostasis). This resistance stage essentially reverses the processes described in the alarm stage. Here the body attempts to adapt itself to a state of calm and tranquility.

Exhaustion Stage. When a period of intense stress lasts longer than six to eight weeks, the body enters the exhaustion stage. Sometimes this exhaustion is referred to as "burnout." What this means is that your supply of energy is depleted and your ability to withstand stress is lowered.

How you respond to a stressful event is determined by how you interpret it. In other words, stress is an individual matter. While two individuals may experience the same stressor, their responses may vary. Evan and James, two teenage boys, have accidentally locked their keys in their cars. Let's look at their responses.

Evan and James

When Evan notices that his keys are missing, he retraces his steps and finds his keys locked in the car. He is annoyed that he will have to use his lunch hour to try to retrieve his keys, or to call his mother at work and wait for her to bring the extra set to him. Also, he is worried about the inconvenience that he might cause her, but he doesn't become upset.

When James sees that his keys are missing, he has a totally different reaction. He frantically asks his friends if they have seen his keys and gets irritated when they don't become involved in helping him locate the missing keys. Unable to think of anything else but locating the keys, he forgets to get necessary books and materials from his locker before his next class. For the next three hours he cannot concentrate on his school activities. He is demanding and impatient with his friends, and short and unfriendly toward his teachers. He gets a headache and a nauseous feeling in his stomach. His whole day is shot.

Each young man encounters the same stressful event, but it's James' reaction to the event that produces the debilitating result.

Everyone Fears Something: What Causes You Stress?

Just as important as knowing what stress is, is knowing what causes you stress. Can you identify your stressors? I'll bet you thought you were the only one who had stress! Not so; everyone does. Here are the more common stressors and fears listed by young adults at each grade level.

Fifth Grade:
- Fear of being chosen first on any team (and being made "an example")
- Fear of losing a best friend
- Fear that a friend will share your "secrets" with someone else
- Fear of not being able to do schoolwork and being embarrassed by classmates

Sixth Grade:
- Fear of the change your growing body is undergoing
- Fear of not passing into middle school/junior high
- Fear of peer disapproval
- Fear that you don't look like the other students
- Fear of not being liked by the other students

Seventh Grade:

- Fear of being selected first (and having to lead) and fear of being picked last (interpreted as being disliked or unpopular)
- Fear of your sexuality (peers have shared wild stories — you wonder whether to believe them or not)
- Concern about your emotional happiness/unhappiness
- Fear of not being able to do schoolwork and being embarrassed by other classmates

Eighth Grade:

- Fear of being selected last (seen as being disliked or unpopular)
- Fear of sexuality (not enough information to keep up with all the changes you're experiencing)
- Concern about emotional happiness/unhappiness
- Fear of activities, such as physical education, that require you to expose your body to peers

Ninth Grade:

- Fear of others judging your sexuality (name-calling)
- Fear of activities that require you to expose your body
- Concern about emotional happiness/unhappiness
- Fear of being challenged to a confrontation (getting into a fight)

Tenth Grade:

- Fear of being disliked or unpopular
- Fear that another peer will vie for your "sweetheart"
- The feeling that you aren't enjoying school or doing well there ("I'm not a good student," "I don't do well in school, but I don't know why.")
- Concern about harmony in relationships (especially in your family)
- Fear that you aren't in a good family (feeling that other families have it more together than yours does)

Eleventh Grade:

- Fear of "not being OK"
- Fear of being ridiculed by class members
- Fear of not having enough money
- Fear that other adults will interpret your roles for you as you try on and define your own values
- Concern over not knowing what you want to do in life

Twelfth Grade:

- Fear that other adults will interpret your life for you (you want to clarify your goals and values for yourself)

- Fear of not knowing what to do next year (life outside of school)
- Fear that you didn't learn anything in school ("I just didn't take school seriously," "I don't think I learned anything," "I don't think I'll make it in a college or career.")

When you understand your fears, you're more likely to find workable solutions. Being able to manage stress helps you to develop confidence in yourself and in your ability to meet challenges head on, thus strengthening your self-esteem. The examples shown below are typically stressful for most people. Read each one and in the spaces provided add some of your own.

I feel stressed when:

- My parents are really upset with me.
- I have an argument with my best friend.
- I don't have enough money for the things I would like.
- I feel my appearance is not what I want it to be.
- I have too much to do and not enough time to do it.
- I don't know what to do in a given situation.
- I loan money to friends who don't repay it.
- A friend tells a shared secret to others or betrays me.
- _____
- _____
- _____
- _____

How Does Stress Affect You?

The effects of stress show up in three ways: physically, emotionally, and behaviorally. Shown below are some of the effects of stress in each of these three categories. Does stress affect you in any of these ways? Read each example and in the spaces provided list other ways you are affected by stress.

Stress affects me **physically.** For example:

- My muscles get tense.
- My hands get cold or sweaty.
- My stomach feels as if it is churning.
- I have difficulty sleeping.
- My heart beats rapidly.
- I have sudden bursts of energy.
- I am extremely tired.
- I lose my appetite, or eat too much.

58 YOU & SELF-ESTEEM

- _____
- _____
- _____
- _____

Stress affects me **emotionally**. For example:

- I get nervous.
- I cry or want to hit out or strike something.
- I feel sad, or giggle a lot.
- I worry excessively.
- I am irritable or feel depressed.
- I feel bad about myself.
- I daydream a lot at school (or have bad dreams at night).
- I get angry easily.
- I lose interest in my appearance.

- _____
- _____
- _____
- _____

Stress affects my **behavior**. For instance:

- I have difficulty concentrating.
- I use food, drugs, or alcohol as a way of coping.
- I use attention-getting antics.
- I become grouchy, irritable, blaming, or sarcastic with family or friends.
- I become abrasive or get into fights.
- I may not tell the truth about something.
- I get into arguments or fights with others.
- I deliberately do subpar work (not caring about how it is done).

- _____
- _____
- _____
- _____

How Do You Cope With Your Stress?

When you are able to cope, you feel "in charge." Being in charge gives you the confidence to handle the situation. No one likes feeling out of control or powerless. How do you cope in stressful situations? Some young people cope by tuning out, running from, or otherwise avoiding the situation. Others cope by hanging in there when they hit the rough times and facing the stressful situation head on. How about you? Do you deal with stressful situations in a positive (effective) way?

The best way to manage a stressful event is before it gets completely out of hand. When one event is allowed to lead to another, the result is a cycle of stress.

THE STRESS CYCLE

As you read about Rob's day, think about whether many of the things that happened to Rob have also happened to you on your "bad" days. See if you can find reasonable clues to the following questions:

- What went wrong here?
- How did one unfortunate event lead to another?
- Could Rob have stopped some of the problems from occurring? How?
- What coping strategies could he have used to help him better manage his day?

Rob's Day

1. It's Wednesday. Rob sets his alarm for 7:00 a.m. but it fails to go off. He awakens at 7:35. Because Rob is running late he skips breakfast, forgets to feed the dog, and doesn't make up his room.

2. Rob dashes for the bus, but because he is late, he misses it. Luckily for Rob, his father has not yet left for work. Rob asks for a ride to school. Reluctantly, his father agrees to take him. Since this will take his father out of his way, he, too, will be late for an appointment; he's annoyed at Rob because this is the second time this week that Rob has missed the bus. They ride to school in silence. This makes Rob painfully aware of how unhappy his father is with him.

3. Because Rob arrives late to school he must go to the office to get a late-pass before he can be admitted to class. Suddenly Rob remembers that because his father was in a bad mood he didn't ask his father to write out an explanation for the tardiness. Afraid to call his father, and because he's unable to get a pass, Rob now must sit out first hour in the office.

4. Since he was without a pass and absent from first-hour class, Rob missed the science test. His teacher says he will not allow Rob to make up the test since he had an unexcused absence. This makes Rob really upset because he needed that test to improve upon his grade point average in order to keep his eligibility for the tennis team. He is the captain of the team and being removed because of low grades will be an embarrassment. Besides, his dad has promised to pay half on a car for Rob if his grades improve by the end of this semester. Thinking about not being able to purchase a car makes Rob angry.

5. Rob goes to his locker to get his books for second-hour class. Searching for his math book, he discovers it missing. His lockermate has inadvertently picked up Rob's book instead of his own. Rob is frantic. When Rob failed to turn in his math assignment yesterday, his teacher warned him not to let it happen again. Now this overdue math paper is in

the book his lockermate has, and Rob has no idea where he could be. Rather than face the teacher, Rob decides to skip math class today.

6. Rob's math teacher takes attendance. Because Rob is not reported on the absence lists, the vice-principal calls his mother at work to inform her that her son is not in school.

7. The bell rings and Rob heads off to third-hour class. When friends tease him about his whereabouts during second hour, he is rude to them. Being upset with his friends makes him feel uneasy.

8. Rob is standing in the lunch line when he notices his lockermate. "Hey Johnson! You took my math book, you idiot!" Rob calls out. Barney Johnson, who isn't having such a hot day either, calls Rob a bad name. Rob shoves his lockermate against the wall and is ready to hit him when the vice-principal stops him. Surprised to see Rob, the principal tells Rob about the call he made earlier to his mother.

9. Feeling really frustrated, Rob shouts at the vice-principal, demanding that he be allowed to stay in line and have lunch.

10. As he's led to the office, Rob thinks about what the vice-principal has in mind for him. He is also worried about the phone call the vice-principal made to his mother. Knowing his mother has been informed that he's not in school makes him feel even more anxious. He knows she will call his father to tell him. He asks if he can use the phone in the office to call his mom, but is reminded that students cannot use the office phone. Rob is not allowed to leave the office now that he's in trouble for fighting, so he is unable to place a call to her from the hall pay phone.

11. Finally, at 3:15 the school day is over.

Whew! Rob has had a pretty tense day, don't you think? Of course, you could write your own stress cycle script using events from your own life. Notice how one event seems to lead to another. What happens to you when an unpleasant event occurs and you aren't able to get in control or stop other events from following? Can you see, as in the example with Rob, how each event influences and often provokes the next one?

Understanding how one event leads to another is the first step in learning ways to cope effectively with stress. By learning how to make stress work for you rather than letting it cause you to get completely out of control, you increase your self-esteem.

TO DO . . .

1. List as many of your fears as you can think of. These can be serious or silly, real or imagined. The goal is to brainstorm and get them all down on paper.

■ _____

_____

Emotional Security: What Do You Get Stressed Out About? 61

■ _____
_____

■ _____
_____

■ _____
_____

Now go back through the list and see how many of your fears actually came true. For example, if you're afraid of being rejected by a friend when you ask him or her to go to a special event with you, think of whether or not that actually happened. If you did get turned down, remember how nice the boy or girl was about it and how you did in fact manage to survive the rejection. Even if the boy or girl was not nice, did you handle their rejection in a positive way? For example, think about the book you are afraid to return to the library because it is late. Did you really get into all that much trouble when you finally returned it? The key is to see that your fears, while perhaps real, are not the end of the world.

2. Describe a time when fear kept you from doing something you desperately wanted to do. Perhaps you wanted to try out for the cheerleading squad but thought you were too clumsy or not popular enough. How did you feel about yourself when you didn't even make the effort? Now imagine that you did go through with it. Play out two scenarios: one in which you succeeded and one in which you failed. How did you feel about yourself in each case? Did you respect yourself more for trying?

_____
_____
_____
_____
_____

3. Describe a time when you saw someone who obviously was petrified and forcing herself to complete a task. Perhaps you heard a singer whose voice was shaky and whose hands were white-knuckled from being gripped so tightly together. Think of how you felt when she was done with the performance. Maybe you pitied her during the task, but didn't you admire her when she was done? What is the biggest fear you have overcome?

_____

_____

_____

_____

_____

_____

TO THINK ABOUT...

1. How can fears make you feel awful about yourself? What is the connection between being afraid and thinking you are not worthy or capable?

2. Who can help you deal with your fears? Do you have a support group of parents, teachers, friends you can go to? Is it better to try to tough it out on your own and not admit your fear, or try to get help? Will people think less of you if you admit you are frightened?

3. How can you force yourself to stop a fear before it grows and overwhelms you? Do you find yourself carrying fears from one day to the next, allowing them to fester and grow, perhaps to ruin your whole week? How can you deal with such long-term fears, especially if they have a basis in fact (such as being concerned about physical safety)?

ated. # UNIT IV

IDENTITY

CHAPTER 10

IDENTITY: How Unique Do You Think You Really Are?

The Nature of Being a Person

The more we learn about how we grow and change throughout each year of life — of what it's like being two or five, six or nine, eleven or seventeen — the more we learn about the nature of being a person. Each age or stage of life differs. At age fourteen a young person's primary need is for unconditional acceptance of himself as an individual. He wants to be accepted, no matter what. Long hair, green hair, or shaved hair, his actions will center on gaining approval and total acceptance for his individual sense of self from parents, teachers, and peers. We call this necessary and natural "developmental" stage, seeking *autonomy*. In contrast, a five-year-old wants to be with his parents all the time and worries about their safety when he's away from them. Being without his parents — his greatest fear — causes him distress. We call this necessary and natural stage separation *anxiety*. Whereas the fourteen-year-old seeks separation from his parents, the five-year-old frets over it.

The particular stage of development that you are experiencing is one of the driving forces behind your actions and is reflected in your behavior. In other words, you're not such a mystery after all: It's fairly easy to tell what's going to be important to you this year, next year, and the next! Does that surprise you? I'll bet you thought no one knew you or understood you, but in fact, just like a two-year-old is a lot like other two-year olds, twelve-year-olds are pretty much like twelve-year-olds, and sixteen-year-olds are pretty much like sixteen-year-olds!

By being aware of these stages, you can better understand yourself, and consequently, your behavior. Best of all, because you won't be such a mystery or puzzle to yourself, you can learn and apply the best ways of coping with your life at each stage.

The Work of Growing Up

Each stage of your development has its own set of tasks, each one focused on self-knowledge. The work of each stage is fairly well defined. I'll give you a general overview to help you see how each stage influences your perception of self. The suggested reading section at the back of this book provides additional resources, and you may wish to ask your counselor or librarian for further suggestions. Nothing can be more exciting than learning about you!

I'm going to begin with age two, then give you the highlights of what's involved at age three and four just to help you see how each stage relates to the other. From there I'll describe the characteristics of five more key stages. If you want, you can jump ahead and read about your stage, then come back to the rest to see how each builds on the other.

Stages and Their Tasks

Age Two: Autonomy. Up until the age of two a child primarily views himself as part of his mother or father. Upon reaching two he becomes aware that he is separate from them. The two words that best describe his new-found selfhood, the awareness that he is in fact a separate person, are "No" and "Mine!" Possession is a tool he uses to enforce that sense of a separate self.

So what does that mean? It does not mean that the two-year-old is a selfish, mean little child. Rather, he's looking for power and ways to assert it. Helping this child develop a sense of self is a matter of allowing him power and ways to be safely assertive. He needs choices. For example, let him pick out which shoes he wants to wear or how he wants to comb his hair. Let him decide which book you are going to read to him. In each instance provide him with two or three choices, all of which you can live with.

When we understand this child's needs, we can see that this stage lays the foundation for him being able to value himself. Through his "work" he learns that he can count on his own abilities, to trust that he can assert himself — these traits are the forerunners of independence. If these tasks have been met with a fair degree of success, at age three he will be quite independent and not so insecure that he cries the moment his mom or dad leaves the room.

Age Three: Mastery. Once he realizes his separateness, the three-year-old goes on to master his environment. Mastery plays an important role in his perception of self: It influences his feeling of being capable (or not capable). He needs to feel successful. He labors over each of his accomplishments. He is slow and methodical, and it takes forever to do each task! Because he needs feedback to know if he has been successful, he strives for recognition of these achievements. "Watch me! Watch me!" he says over and over to anyone who will watch! Knowing that he has something to offer nurtures his sense of competence and proves his value — he feels worthwhile.

The search for mastery stimulates curiosity. "Why, why, why?" she wants to know. Her drive for discovering (learning) is unlimited. She explores her surroundings, observes people, and examines how she fits in.

How can this child's need for self-esteem be met? By answering her repeated questions, recognizing her achievements (for example, putting up her drawings where they are visible), repeating things she has said, showing her that you have listened to her, and asking her to tell you again about something she enjoys discussing, such as how or why she has drawn a certain picture, or why she has chosen to use certain colors in the picture.

Age Four: Initiative. The four-year-old's task is developing self-initiative — the forerunner of self-responsibility. This may involve something as simple as taking responsibility for putting his toys away after he's done playing with them, as detailed as making his own bed — complete with crooked sheets, lumpy covers and corners — or as complex as learning to tie his shoelaces. What's most important to him is that he's taken it upon himself to do a task — to attempt it, to strive. Initiative is the forerunner of motivation.

The implications for developing self-esteem mean that this child's attempts should remain exactly as completed by him. Focus praise not on the way the task was done, but on the fact that it was attempted and/or completed. If you want him to improve the way he does a particular task, show him rather than tell him. Experience, not words, is his best teacher now. This will encourage further displays of his initiative while also encouraging self-confidence.

NOTE: As you have been reading this material, have you been thinking about anyone in particular? Maybe the part about "Watch me! Watch me!" reminded you of the time you wanted your mother to watch you jump off the diving board. Perhaps as you read you chuckled, remembering something your brother or sister did at that age. The best way to make this material memorable to you and to understand it completely, is to associate it with people you know. Think as you go through each age group of someone you know who acts or acted just like that. While we are all individuals, it's interesting to note how much alike we are within certain guidelines.

Age Ten: Who Are People? Ten-year-olds like approval, direction, and affirmation from both adults and peers. Though outwardly this young person may claim contempt for the opposite sex, he or she probably has a secret boyfriend or girlfriend (who may not even know it!). Games of boys chasing girls or vice-versa are common. This is the time for learning about acceptance from others and of discovering maleness (or femaleness).

Age Eleven to Twelve: Regrouping and Taking Stock. This is a comparatively mellow time, placed between two major periods of intense growth. It's a time for refining physical abilities and academic competence as well as deciding what's important (meaningful) and what isn't. It's a period of trying on many different roles to see which ones feel right. In this stage you are observing everything because you are deciding who you would like to be like and what that means.

Ages Thirteen to Fifteen: Go for It! All systems are on Go! here. Your need to be physical and your curiosity and ability to expand your understanding of the intellectual, social, and spiritual realms are remarkable. You want to know about everything and everyone. It's a time of enormous growth in every way: one more stage is being left behind, and adolescence is being born. When viewing the scope of tasks that must be undertaken at this stage, it's no wonder that it's also a time of chaos for you. Building a solid sense of self and personal worth at this time is probably the toughest and most important task you have ever faced. All learning seems to be a process of trial and error. You learn as much from what doesn't work as from what does!

One of the most difficult and trying tasks is coping with your (physical) growing pains. Physical maturation — internal and external — occurs at an amazing rate. Key hormones are at work now, doing their job of moving you from preadolescence to full-scale puberty. The awkwardness of physical growth is coupled with sometimes feeling lonely and alone. The fact that boys are about two years behind girls in physical development doesn't help.

The two-year time span in development will even leave some girls out of sync with other girls, causing each to question just why she is (or isn't) growing in a particular way.

Age Sixteen: "Excuse Me, but You're in My Way!" There really is no other age like this one. It's not uncommon for you to experience feelings of being confused, embarrassed, guilty, awkward, inferior, ugly, and scared, all in the same day. In fact, you can swing from childish and petulant behaviors to being sedate, or acting rational or irrational, all in the same class hour. You swing from intellectual to giddy — back and forth — as you try to figure out just who you are and what's going on with you. It's a time of confusion and uncertainty. Often these swings come complete with easy tears and genuine sobs, high-level, indepth sensitivity, great insights and sudden bursts of learning, flare-ups of anger, and boisterous and unfounded giggles. Changes in your hormones create ups and downs as well as sexual feelings. The self-esteem need at this age is to belong. The task is to learn about yourself as a sexual being and how you are perceived by the opposite sex.

This is a time of duality: You want to be with others yet you want to be alone; you need your friends but will sabotage them if they appear to out do you; you'll root for a friend out loud but secretly wish for her demise. It's a time when you want total independence but by no means are you capable of it; you don't really want to live without your parents, even though you may believe they are a roadblock in your life!

You have a hard time looking ahead and visualizing the long-term effects of your current behaviors — for example, connecting skipping class with not being admitted to college or not studying as cheating yourself out of an education. Today — this very moment — is what matters most to you. Feelings of invulnerability and immortality lead you to behave in reckless ways: The "it-can't-happen-to-me" attitude prevails as some young people drive too fast, engage in sexual experiences, and experiment with alcohol and drugs. This is truly a time of identity crisis — an age of frustration.

Ages Seventeen to Eighteen: Establishing Independence. The final stage of childhood is establishing total independence. In looking beyond being dependent on others to dependence on self, you confront some rather big (and frightening) issues. The three tasks that confront young people in this age group are:

1. Determining your vocation. "What am I going to do (for work) with my life?" "Can I support myself?" Answering these questions gives life meaning. Underlying this task is the self-esteem need to be somebody, to experience positive feelings of strength, power, and competence.

2. Establishing your values. The goal is to sort out your own values and to decide which ones to keep and which ones to discard. This is the only way you can develop integrity within yourself. It's time for you to establish a workable and meaningful philosophy of life, to search for your own personal beliefs, and to face religious, ethical, and value-laden ideologies — on your own. Developing personal convictions will be influenced by your level of self-esteem — especially if there is conflict between what your parents raised you to believe and what your friends find acceptable. Will you claim and stay committed to what is true for you? As you ponder the thought, you will grasp and cling to sweeping idealisms as you try some on for size.

3. Establishing your self-reliance. The goal here is to depend on yourself — independence. Accomplishing this task develops self-trust and confidence. Underlying this task is the self-esteem need to be yourself — to define yourself by your own values, and to see through your own lens, and not through the role of student, athlete, son, and so on.

Your identity is critical to your self-esteem. Who you think you are determines how you feel about yourself, which in turn determines how hard you work, how motivated you are, how high you set your goals. By understanding the various characteristics of the age groups and the process of development in each, you are better able to understand that certain behaviors and feelings are normal, and to accept them as simply a part of growing up. It can also help you to change what you don't like about yourself, and learn a better way.

TO DO . . .

1. Think about a particular stage of growth and write a brief description of how you acted at that age, for example, when you were beginning first grade. Describe yourself at that stage. How does it feel to "look back" to a particular stage? How have you changed?

_____
_____
_____
_____
_____
_____

2. What "age" are you most looking forward to, and why?

_____
_____
_____

3. Do you enjoy your present stage of development? Explain?

TO THINK ABOUT...

1. Is there a fundamental difference between boys and girls at different stages? Is this difference normal and acceptable, or do teachers, friends, siblings, or others make too big a deal out of it and set up stereotypical behaviors that can be sexist and counter-productive?

2. Does knowing the characteristics of a stage help or hurt a child who is going through it? For example, does knowing that a sixteen-year-old has hysterical mood swings make him or her easier to live with, or does a sixteen-year-old become discouraged knowing that perhaps the worst is yet to come?

3. Do developmental stages end with adulthood, or are there stages that adults go through as well? Is self-esteem influenced by changes as an adult, or is it pretty well determined in childhood?

CHAPTER 11

IDENTITY: Answering the "Who Am I?" Question

Uncovering the Real You

As you read this poem called "The Paint Brush" by Lee Ezell, think about the ways in which you may be trying to keep others from knowing who you really are.

> I keep my paint brush with me
> Wherever I may go,
> In case I need to cover up
> So the real me doesn't show.
> I'm so afraid to show you me,
> Afraid of what you'll do
> You might laugh or say mean things
> I'm afraid I might lose you.
> I'd like to remove all of my paint coats
> To show you the real, true me,
> But I want you to try and understand
> I need you to like what you see.
> So if you'll be patient and close your eyes
> I'll strip off all my coats real slow,
> Please understand how much it hurts
> To let the real me show.
> Now my coats are all stripped off
> I feel naked, bare and cold,
> If you still love me with all that you see
> You are my friend pure as gold.
> I need to save my paint brush though
> And hold it in my hand,
> I want to keep it handy
> In case somebody doesn't understand.
> So please protect me, my dear friend
> And thanks for loving me true,
> But please let me keep my paint brush with me
> Until I love me, too.

Have you ever felt that your friends, teachers, or parents see you one way, but you see yourself differently than they do? Have you felt that sometimes you had to cover up the "real you" and act like who you thought they wanted you to be? Most of us feel that way from time to time, but you certainly don't want to mask the real you. Yet many young people feel they have to. With so many people to please, each one wanting something different from you (parents, teachers, friends, coaches), you may wonder "What about *me*? What do *I* want? Who am *I*?"

WHO ARE YOU?

What Is Your Identity?

It's not a question of "finding an identity." We all have an identity. The question is, what do you see, and is this image a healthy, positive one? Sometimes it is, and sometimes it isn't. Does your personal price tag read "damaged goods" or "valuable merchandise?" How you answer this question is important because — accurate or inaccurate, healthy or dysfunctional — this inner picture of self-worth influences your actions. If you see yourself in a positive light, you act positively; if you see yourself as a problem child, you're usually getting in trouble.

Very few of us have a perfect inner picture. There is always something we can do to feel better about ourselves, to enhance our self-esteem. Sometimes the inner picture is basically strong and needs only to be fine tuned. At other times, the picture is so confused that it needs to be reworked entirely. The goal of this chapter is to help you identify that inner picture and see it clearly.

The Actual, Ideal, and Public Selves

To answer the question, Who am I? let's look through three windows that will show you three versions of yourself. These three views, when combined, will give you a sense of your identity. We call these the actual, ideal, and public selves.

The actual self is a composite picture of how successful you feel in each of your many roles — student, friend, son, daughter, brother, sister, paperboy, babysitter, and so on. It's your overall picture of how you interact in each of these roles and how you are treated in each of them in return. For example, you may feel like a successful student but not very comfortable with your ability to make and keep friends, or you may feel good about your associations with friends but not so good in your role as a student.

The ideal self is made up of your aspirations. It's the ideal of how you would like to be and whom you want to become — the striving. Have you ever said (or thought): "I wish I were prettier, friendlier, an A student, thinner (heavier), smarter." Maybe you are more definite, saying, "I want to be a member of the baseball team, a lifeguard, or make lots of money." It's your answer to, "If I could do anything I want . . ." or "When I'm grown up . . ." and your belief in someday having or being those things.

The public self is the image you are willing to show to others. It's putting up a good front or disclosing only a certain image to others, a slice of who you really are. You can decide what this will be, or you can be influenced by what others want you to be (popular, mean, spirited and so on), or you can base this self on whom you imagine they want you to be.

When these three "selves" are out of balance you don't know who you are or what you stand for — you're in turmoil. If you're acting primarily from your public self, for example, you may think you have to be popular. If so, your actions are focused primarily on gaining other people's attention and feedback.

Each of us forms a picture of ourselves in each of these three areas. What's important is that this picture be in perspective. If your life projects mainly the public self, for example, you can easily lose sight of how the other areas help to keep you safe. We can see this imbalance magnified in the lives of people such as John Belushi. Belushi's public self was that of a clown and a slob, like the character he played in "Animal House." He put up a front of being a happy, exuberant guy, rather crass, uncaring, insensitive. The public was willing to accept him as such. They were less willing to accept him as a sensitive, romantic man. When Belushi tried to play a suave hero in "Continental Divide," the public refused to accept him in this role. The public had decided on the front it would accept and couldn't handle any deviation from that. Belushi, like most of us, probably considered that he had more to offer than just a slapstick act. It must have been very difficult for him to know that the public refused to see any more to the man than that front. Belushi's self-identity became more and more tied up in one self-window to the exclusion of the others. A toll is exacted for having a life out of balance.

How do your actual, ideal and public selves differ?

Who Are You?

What is your sense of identity? The following questions can help you conduct an assessment. Answer each one carefully.

1. How do I see myself? What four words best describe me?

_____   _____

_____   _____

2. What four words best describe how I would like to be?

_____   _____

_____   _____

3. How do others see me? What four words would they use to describe me?

_____   _____

_____   _____

4. In what ways are my "three selves" alike?

_____

_____

5. In what ways do my "three selves" differ?

_____

_____

THE IMPORTANCE OF APPEARANCE

Appearance is another important part of your sense of identity. Did you know that children begin to form a concept of themselves (and others) based on "outer beauty" and to differentiate between what they consider to be "attractive and unattractive" at about three years of age? Children actually stereotype others on the basis of physical attractiveness, which can be defined as a generally neat and clean appearance. That's all! But look how much appearance affects their self-esteem. Attractive children are looked at, smiled at, touched, asked to play, and named as "best friends" more often than other children. These children receive the most positive numbers of eye contacts by teachers and garner the most positive strokes (reinforcements) in the classroom. Such children receive a good share of positive attention, a plus in helping them cope with the normal frustrations of learning, and of course, in feeling good about themselves. Positive attention, stroking, touching, and verbal and nonverbal affirmations are the very factors that contribute to helping students achieve.

I'm not saying that clothes don't count because obviously they do. When someone wears something striking or looks great in a certain outfit, naturally we want to look at them — they get our attention. We also know that young people who do not dress like everyone else, and that includes those who are overdressed in comparison with other students, feel different and have negative feelings about themselves. That's one reason why so many private schools request that students wear uniforms and many of the public schools have dress codes. Dressing alike puts students on an equal footing in this one area. Here are some key questions for you to think about in assessing your appearance:

- How does my overall appearance compare to that of my friends (and classmates)?
- Am I clean and well-groomed each day?
- Am I overdressed?
- How do I feel about my appearance?
- How would others describe my appearance?

Clearly, physical attributes influence what you think about yourself and others. Since society places such an enormous emphasis on outward physical appearance, there's a lot of pressure to look "hot," as you say. Just remember, we can't all (and shouldn't want to) be Madonnas!

The important thing to remember is that you don't need exciting "packaging" to be accepted. Think back to third grade: Do you remember who was the best-dressed kid in your class? Probably not, but I'll bet you can remember who was your best friend, or even who was the class bully. Self-esteem is more important in the long run. Not all of your self-perceptions come from the way you look! But since some of them do, and since you now know that having a generally clean and neat appearance is an important part of these perceptions, keep yourself well-groomed and clean.

How Your Body Image Affects Your Self-Esteem

As I travel around the country and speak to youth groups, I frequently ask, "Who are you? How would you describe yourself?" Youths of all ages automatically respond with statements about their physical being. "I'm 5'4", have green eyes, brown hair . . ." When I ask, "If you could change anything about yourself, what would it be?" again, most kids, regardless of age, will cite some characteristic of their physical being. "I wouldn't want to be so tall (or short)," or something to that effect.

In an earlier chapter we looked at the importance of health and fitness and your caring enough not to assault your body with drugs or alcohol. Another sense of your identity is gained by relating to your physical self and then sometimes comparing that physical self to others. Throughout the stages of childhood as you grow and develop, the body makes a number of growth spurts. At times these changes are minor: A ten-year-old girl may gain four to six pounds and grow one to two inches within a 12- to 14-month period. A ten-year-old boy will gain six to eight pounds and gain two to three inches in height. Sometimes these changes are dramatic: On the average, a thirteen-year-old girl will gain 14 to 25 pounds and grow about three to five inches during a 12-month period; a fifteen-year-old boy will gain 10 to 15 pounds and some 10 to 12 inches in height. In other words, each year of life brings about its own set of growth demands. Such changes create a new self-image for you.

In addition to outer physical growth, internal organs enlarge and mature in their functioning and a number of hormones are set in motion to trigger body development and maturity. In addition, there are chemical changes in the brain, which produce their own behavioral side-effects. You feel these changes inwardly and compare yourself to others outwardly. With each stage of growth and development a "new" (not always improved!) you emerges. As Becky, a ninth-grader in Michigan, said to me, "Will the real me please stand up and stay around for longer than a few months! I can't keep up with these constant (body) changes, and I'm not so sure I can handle my constantly changing moods, either!"

Building a Positive Sense of Identity

How can you build a positive sense of identity when you are in such a constant state of change? Here are some suggestions.

1. Always speak positively about yourself. When you speak positively about yourself, you impart the message that self-respect matters — you count. When others hear you say, "I respect myself," they are more likely to respect you too. When you are positive, others are happy to be around you; they seek out your company because they enjoy being positive about themselves. This makes you more popular, happier, and more positive . . . and so the cycle continues. You determine your outlook; you create your reality.

2. Respect your fitness and wellness. Take the time to learn how to achieve and maintain good health. Accurate information on nutrition, exercise, rest, and relaxation is crucial.

3. Gain insight into your stage of growth and development. This self-knowledge can prevent many of the destructive behaviors we see youths imposing upon themselves. For example, seventh- and eighth-grade girls are serious offenders in using diet pills, and often engage in bulemic and anorexic behaviors as a way to control the normal weight gain associated with this stage of development. You can imagine why girls become alarmed: In prior stages they see only slight increases in growth and weight from year to year, then all of a sudden they experience a dramatic weight gain. A girl looks in the mirror and says, "How did I get to be so fat and so ugly so fast." Her perception is a very negative one. When a girl is not emotionally ready for these dramatic changes — when she has "perception warp" of the image she sees in the mirror — she can get into some serious negative and self-destructive behaviors aimed at controlling her weight.

4. You are not your looks. Realize that while appearance is important, there is more to your identity than just looks. While you want to be neat and clean and attractive, remember that identity goes beyond image; your intelligence, your sense of humor, your kindness are all attributes of identity. Accept yourself as a total package and appreciate yourself for more than just looks.

TO DO . . .

1. How do students at your school group themselves? How many are "jocks, party animals, brains, nerds," and so on? What effect does belonging to a particular group have on them? What qualities make a student a member of each group?

_____

_____

_____

_____

_____

_____

2. How differently do your friends see you from how you see yourself? Is the different perspective healthy or detrimental?

_____

_____

_____

_____

_____

_____

3. Think of a student who has recently undergone a change of appearance (lost weight, dyed hair). How has his or her sense of self changed and how has this affected his or her behavior (and school performance)?

_____

_____

_____

_____

_____

_____

4. Think of a student whose ideal self and public self differ. How can you help him act as the ideal self?

_____

_____

_____

_____

_____

_____

TO THINK ABOUT...

1. With a group of four or five friends, draw each other's names out of a hat. Write up a description of the person whose name you drew without mentioning her physical characteristics. How many of you can identify the person being described?

2. Have each friend write up what her ideal self would be. Draw the descriptions out of a hat and read them out loud. Can you match the description with the writer? How different are the ideal selves from the way the people see themselves now?

3. Intentionally change your image for just one day. If you are usually a jock, dress in a much more formal style. Notice how differently people treat you. What does this say about your public self and how it affects your self-esteem?

CHAPTER 12

IDENTITY: How Much Are You Influenced by Others?

The Influence of Others on Your Self-Esteem

While one key in answering the "Who am I?" question has to do with wanting to feel unique, special, and different from others, we also need and want to be like them. At all ages we are very much influenced by what others think of us and how they react to us. Sometimes, though, we're too much influenced by them. When this happens, we need to create a picture of ourselves based on our strengths. Colleen learned that the person she is was sometimes hidden under all the layers of other people's expectations.

Colleen's Story

Colleen has an older sister, Heather, who is very pretty and smart. Colleen grew up considering herself "Heather's younger sister" and thinking she was not as smart or as pretty as Heather. When Heather went away to college, Colleen's family moved to a new town. Colleen began attending a new high school where she was a junior. Suddenly, she didn't have Heather to compare herself to anymore. No one asked her about her sister, no teacher reminded her of how well Heather had done. Colleen began to get a new sense of herself, an identity as Colleen, not as Heather's little sister. She felt free to try new things. For the first time she went out for sports, an area she had always avoided since her older sister was All-City in tennis and Colleen thought she could never compete. Colleen joined the swim team at her new school and while not winning any championships, helped out the team and had a lot of fun. She also took more challenging classes, feeling secure that she didn't have to compete with the memory of her sister. Colleen began to feel more comfortable being herself and to like herself more, which increased her happiness. Other students noticed and wanted to be around a person who was always so cheerful. Expressing herself more clearly made her life seem more fun.

We know that a young person with a poorly constructed identity is frequently influenced by others. Not believing in himself, he often conforms to or mimics others and uses negative statements when describing himself. Lacking confidence, he is overly dependent and all too anxious to please other people. He is even willing to misbehave in order to attract attention! He is uncomfortable with praise and likely to deny wrongdoings for fear of rejection. He frequently goes out of his way to be different, such as dressing to extremes to draw attention.

Paul, for example, has begun wearing biker clothing to get attention. He wears a heavy leather jacket, even in the heat, ripped jeans, and a lot of leather jewelry. He looks ridiculous but is willing to put up with the ridicule to be noticed.

A young person with a healthy self-identity, on the other hand, can express individuality without alienating others. He's comfortable accepting praise and makes positive statements about himself and others. He'll stand up for himself. In the presence of peers using drugs, for example, a student is more likely to say, "Hey, I don't do that stuff," something that conveys he's not going to participate, and he'll stay committed to his decision. He can't be easily swayed because he thinks for himself.

Do You Stand Up for Yourself?

Assertiveness skills enable you to assert your rights without intimidating others or being intimidated in return. There are times when you will want to tell others how you feel, what you think is important, and what you can and can't do. You'll need to do so in a way that is accepted by others and that gets your point across effectively. It doesn't do you any good to yell or to let others guess what your needs are. Besides, they'll most likely guess wrong. Then your needs will go unmet and you'll be disappointed because your expectations haven't met with success. It also doesn't do you much good to hope that by your being nice to people they'll somehow know what it is you need and give it to you. Assertiveness skills allow you confidently to confront situations that would typically produce anxiety or frustration, or cause you to deny your feelings.

As you no doubt have learned from experience, some youths learn they can get what they want by shouting, pouting, ridiculing, and intimidating. Others learn that by being sweet, likable, "I'll-do-anything-you-want" types, they can get others to respond to them in the way they want. You want to learn how to assert yourself appropriately. To be assertive means to value yourself — to act with confidence and authority.

Assertion is "owning" what you need and not putting the responsibility for that ownership on someone else. Assertion is communicating in such a way that others will listen to and not be offended by what you say. It's giving another person the opportunity to respond in return. It's a manner that is direct, self-respecting, and straightforward. Here are some nonverbal and verbal ways to do that.

1. Eye contact. The assertive person will have direct eye contact. This means you look the other person in the eye (not staring) and hold the contact fairly steadily throughout the conversation.

2. Hand gestures. Use hand gestures to help you emphasize the content and importance of what you're saying.

3. Posture. Posture can also indicate assertiveness: sit or stand straight when communicating, shoulders back, head up.

4. Voice. Speaking up and not mumbling is being assertive. Sometimes you hear a person make an assertive comment and then ruin the effect by either dropping or raising his voice at the end. For example, "I want you to be more truthful with me" sounds fine by itself. However, if instead of waiting for a response he says, "Okay?" the assertiveness of the statement is lost. Other phrases that can detract from assertiveness (particularly when delivered in a whiny voice) are, "You know?" or "You know what I mean?" Being assertive involves knowing when to stop talking.

5. Owning your statements. One hallmark of assertive behavior is the making of I statements, such as: "I feel," "I like," "I wish," "I would appreciate," "I need." The passive person puts responsibility on someone else, often finishing a statement by asking, "Don't you think so?" or "Is that okay?"

To get your needs met assertively you must learn to communicate in a direct and straightforward fashion that does not cause anyone else duress. People respect honesty, even criticism, if it's presented in an open, honest, and kind way. Statements that affirm what you are feeling and what you need represent a way of taking responsibility for yourself.

TO DO . . .

How good are you at communicating your needs? Do you let others know how you're feeling? Here are some questions to test your ability to stand your ground.

1. A girl asks to cut in front of you in a line. You don't want to let her cut. What do you say?

_____

_____

_____

2. A classmate asks to copy your answers to a test. You don't want him to. What do you say?

_____

_____

_____

3. The teacher asks the entire class to stay after school because someone was talking. You don't want to take the blame for something you know isn't your fault. What do you do?

_____

_____

_____

4. What can you do if another student is calling you names?

_____

Identity: How Much Are You Influenced by Others?   81

5. You don't understand a problem the teacher has just explained. What would you say in asking for help?

6. Your mother is in the car honking the horn for you to hurry so she can get you to school. You have not fed and watered your dog yet. What can you do?

7. Your teacher has returned your homework, and you notice that she has marked an answer wrong that you are sure is correct. What do you do?

8. You really like one of your classmates, but another classmate tells you not to "hang around" with her because she is weird. What do you do and/or say?

9. You trip and fall. Someone calls you clumsy. What do you do or say?

10. You agree to meet a friend every day to ride bikes to school and you forget. What do you do? What do you say to your friend when you see him?

11. Someone says you lied when you didn't. What do you do or say?

TO THINK ABOUT...

1. Which is more important, the way you feel about yourself or the way others see you? How can you tell what others feel about you? Is it possible for you to change their feelings about you by changing your feelings about yourself?

2. How does your sense of self affect your daily life? How can feeling good and strong make you act differently? Is it ever possible to get to know the real you?

3. How much of an effect does the "outer you" have on the "inner you"? In other words, are you mostly what you look like? If you are wholesome looking or if you look like a biker or a surfer, how much does that determine your identity? Does this change the way others view you?

UNIT V

BELONGING

CHAPTER 13

BELONGING: Your Need for Friendships

Strive for Interdependence

There is an ancient Chinese proverb that says, "Our life is like a piece of paper on which every passerby leaves a mark." Other people are indeed important to us because they help make our lives full and rewarding. We care about belonging, about having a connection to others. This connection is called affiliation. You don't want to cling to others and be totally dependent on them; nor do you want to be aloof and cool and distant, not involved with people at all. A healthy balance between the two, an interdependence, is the ideal.

WHAT GROUPS DO YOU BELONG TO?

Many of us define ourselves by the people in our lives or the groups we are in. For example, we might introduce ourselves to an adult by saying, "I'm Sarah, Alice's daughter." Or you could tell someone you meet at a party, "I'm Ron's sister," or "I'm Margo's best friend." Some people develop a sense of belonging by being a member of a club or a sports team: "I'm a Hawkeye," "I'm on the volleyball team," "I'm a student at school X." Think about where you get your sense of belonging.

1. Family. Of course, the first and most important group we belong to is our family. This can be a small family, just you and your parents and siblings, or a large extended family full of aunts and uncles and cousins. It's important to your sense of self to know that you have a home, people who know the real you and still love and cherish you, people who are always going to be there for you. Even if you argue with your brothers and sisters or get grounded by your parents, you know a firm foundation of love is there. You belong to your family. Even after you leave home and make your own place in the world, you will "come home to the family." Your family gives you a sense of roots.

2. Friends. You may spend more time with your friends than with your family. If your friends and you are at the same school, you probably are with them six or seven hours a day. The groups you belong to, the cliques you join, the people you hang around with help define who you are. You might hang around with the brains or the "cool" kids or the fashion-conscious kids. Although some people say they are loners, even they seem to need to hang out with other loners!

3. Teammates. If you belong to a sports team or a club of some sort, you are a part of a group of teammates. You may not all be good friends away from the court or the field, but on it you are a unit. You take care of, watch out for, and protect each other, and of course, together strive for the win. Even if you don't particularly like someone on your baseball team, you know he will come to your defense if the pitcher throws the ball too close to you, and you'd do the same for him.

4. Neighbors. If you live in an apartment or condominium complex, you probably see a lot of your neighbors when you get the mail or take out the trash. You may have gotten to know neighbors by car pooling with their children, or going trick-or-treating to their homes at Halloween, or trying to sell them cookies or candy during a fundraiser. Whether you are close to your neighbors or not, you are a part of the neighborhood. You belong there; you know it's home.

5. Co-workers. If you are old enough to have a part-time job, you belong to a group of co-workers. You are all on the same team, griping about the boss for fun, competing with other stores or businesses, having a good time just being together, and of course, working toward the mutual goal of completing a certain task or project.

You belong to many different groups, and these groups will be different at different times in your life. For example, when you are very little your family is the main group in your life. As you get older you care more about your teammates and friends. Later your co-workers will take up a lot of your time, or your own family unit. In each instance it's important to recognize how vital that sense of affiliation and belonging is and to nourish it.

"Basketball Bill"

Bill's family teases him and calls him "Basketball Bill" because he spends so much of his time on the courts. If he is not in school, you can find him dribbling a basketball at the neighborhood park. While Bill is pleasant and friendly, he doesn't have any close friends at school. His junior high school doesn't have a basketball team, as it is very small. No one else in the school seems to be as fanatic as Bill is about basketball, so he doesn't get involved with them.

There is a group of kids who go to the park every afternoon and play basketball until it gets too dark to see. They have become Bill's friends. He doesn't have any siblings, and his parents both work, so they aren't home very much. He wouldn't have many other friends if it weren't for the basketball group. Bill knows how lonely he would be if he couldn't hang out with these guys. He needs to know how to strengthen his affiliation with other people. The following suggestions can help him and may be useful to us all in keeping ourselves a part of groups that are important to us.

1. Learn to listen. Listening is a powerful skill because it's a sign of respect. Listening is understanding: This doesn't mean that you necessarily agree with the other person's opinions and ideas but you give him a chance to be heard. It conveys to the other person the message: "My ideas and opinions count. I matter. He cares about me." The next time you're talking observe your listening style. Are you fidgeting and looking restless, or are you showing an interest in what he has to say? Look at the other person and give him your complete attention. Imagine how you would feel if someone didn't listen or pay attention to you. You might feel deflated or irritated or confused.

2. Respect others. Treat all people with respect, even those whom you may feel aren't deserving. Respecting another person is your code of conduct — the way you choose to respond to others. The bottom line is that you must give respect in order to gain respect.

3. Keep commitments and honor your word. If you make and keep promises, over time others see your integrity and learn to trust you. It earns you a reputation as someone worthy of honor.

4. Sincerely apologize when you are wrong. If you've said or done something carelessly or thoughtlessly, have the courage to admit it, to sincerely say: "I was wrong," "I'm sorry." People are usually very forgiving when you acknowledge that you have been unfair. But there's a limit. Apologies lose their meaning when you keep repeating your transgressions. If you embarrass a friend in front of others, acknowledge it, saying, "John, I'm sorry to have embarrassed you the way I did. That was unfair," or "I shouldn't have said that. I didn't mean it and I'm sorry." Then try not to do it again. Remember, you can't talk your way out of something you behaved your way into.

5. Show respect for differences. Develop a tolerance for the differences in others so that you can enjoy a broader range of friendships. Not everyone has the same interests, opinions, feelings, background, or capabilities as you do.

6. Respect others' abilities and show that respect. Show an appreciation for the diversity, talents, and aptitudes of others. Be nonjudgmental. Watch what you say (and how you say it) about others.

7. Foster a sense of comradery rather than competition. You have to be a friend if you want a friend.

ENDING RELATIONSHIPS

Just as you need to know how to make and sustain friendships, you sometimes need to end friendships. There may come a time when you don't want to belong to a certain group anymore. You've probably heard the expression: Don't burn your bridges behind you. This means that you want to be able to ease yourself out of a group without hurting anyone's feelings (any more than is necessary) and without creating ill will or resentment against you that will last.

There are a lot of reasons why you may want to stop belonging to a group. Perhaps you know that the group is toxic rather than good for you. For example, maybe your group is drinking or doing drugs and you're smarter than that. Maybe you just don't like the direction the group is going, like neighborhood friends who want to go to the movies or the arcade all the time when you'd rather put more time into your school studies. Perhaps you've just outgrown your friends, maturing faster than they have. When ending a friendship, end it gently and kindly.

Skills for Ending Friendships

Sixteen-year-old Julie has been asked by Ron to go to the school dance on Friday; however, she has now decided she doesn't want to go out with him. Too embarrassed to call him up and tell him, and lacking the courage to confront him, she decides to stand him up — not to be at home when he comes to pick her up. What else could she have done? Standing up a date is not appropriate; there's a better way to "undo" the date. Here's a way to increase your ability to confront others without backing down once they're on the phone or you meet them face to face. The skill is called *role-playing*. Here's how it works.

Julie and Ron

Test run # 1: (You represent Julie; have a friend represent Ron)

Julie: (pretending to phone Ron) "Hello, Ron?"

Friend: "Hi, Julie!"

Julie: "I'm calling about the dance tomorrow night."

Friend: "Oh, I know! I'm so excited about it! My dad said I could borrow his car instead of using my old beat-up one. Guess what, Julie, I'm taking us to dinner before the dance, and oh, I bought this really great new shirt and sweater in your favorite color! It's going to be so much fun. I'm so excited. I'll pick you up at 6:30."

Julie: (unprepared for Ron's enthusiasm and afraid to disappoint him) "Oh, okay." (She hangs up the phone, really disappointed in herself.) "I don't care, I'm not going out with that nerd!" she yells. "Now I'm stuck with having to go out with him. I'll be so embarrassed. I'm not going to be seen with him. I'm going to the movies instead with Marsha!"

Test run # 2: (You represent Julie; have a friend represent Ron)

Julie: "Hello, Ron?"

Friend: "Hi Julie!"

Julie: "I'm calling about the dance tomorrow night."

Friend: "Oh Julie, I'm glad you called. I'm really sick. I won't be going to school tomorrow, and I won't be able to go to the dance. I'm really sorry. I hope I didn't ruin your weekend plans. Can we talk about it at school on Monday?"

Julie: "I'm sorry to hear you aren't feeling well, Ron. Yes, we can talk next week." (Julie hangs up the phone, surprised, and pleased that she didn't call when she was angry with herself and take it out on him.)

Test run # 3: (You represent Julie; have a friend represent Ron)

Julie: "Hello, Ron?"

Friend: "Hello, Julie!"

Julie: "I'm calling about the dance tomorrow night. I know it's very late to back out, but I really have to. I hope you'll have time to make other plans."

Friend: "Well, I'm sorry to hear that, Julie. I was really looking forward to going. Are you sure I can't change your mind?"

Julie: "Yes, I'm sure, Ron. I really must say no. I'm sorry."

Friend: (sounding disappointed but accepting it) "OK. Bye, Julie. Oh, Julie, if you change your mind, please call me back. OK? Bye."

There are, of course, many more likely responses. But do you see how this kind of rehearsing can help you build confidence in handling situations that have potentially stressful outcomes? As Julie explained when the exercise was over, "Getting practice on how to handle the situation was very helpful to me because I really didn't know how to tell Ron that I had changed my mind about going out with him. To tell you the truth, before I role-played this I was just going to not be home when he came to pick me up for the date. This exercise helped me see how standing him up would have made him feel rejected and humiliated. But you know, I didn't really think I had the nerve to call and cancel, even though there was no way I was going to go out with him. Role-playing gave me the confidence to carry on the conversation I should have had in the first place."

The next phase of Julie's role-playing would be for Julie to reverse roles with Ron, with Julie playing the part of Ron and a male student playing Julie. This would help Julie build confidence in her ability to assert her decision even further. Such planning reduces the likelihood that she will be overwhelmed at the time of confrontation. It also provides Julie with an opportunity to assess her understanding of the situation and test her ability to implement it under stress, such as when Julie really has to confront Ron about breaking the date. And just as importantly, by exchanging roles she gets to put the shoe on the other foot — to put herself in the other person's place.

Learning how to ease yourself in and out of relationships — to interact with others in a positive way — can lead to developing healthy rather than toxic relationships. Groups are a normal, healthy, vital part of our lives. We all need to feel that we fit in somewhere. We all need to have a group of people who smile when they see us coming. A sense of belonging, of affiliation, is part of a strong and healthy sense of self.

TO DO . . .

1. List some of the groups or cliques you belong to. How did you get involved with them? How close are you to those in the group? Are those friends separate from your other friends, or are they all together? How do you show your affiliation (such as by dressing alike)?

_____

_____

_____

2. Describe reasons for joining a group. What are the advantages? Are there any disadvantages? Describe a situation in which a group may no longer be good for you and role-play yourself dropping out of that group.

3. Talk about a time when someone wanted to join a group you were in. Did you let her in? How did you decide? How did you treat her? How did you treat someone you didn't let in?

TO THINK ABOUT...

1. Is it better to belong to a lot of groups or just to one or two special ones? Are you more popular if you belong to several groups, or don't people see you as disloyal if you spread yourself thin like that?

2. Can you ever really go back to a group if you've dropped out of it? How will things be different? Will you feel disloyal for having left, and if so, how will you handle feeling this way?

3. What makes a group good for you and what makes it bad for you? How can you tell when a group that was good turns bad? Are there any warning signs?

4. Can you have a sense of belonging without being friends? Can you belong to a group when the people in it are just schoolmates or acquaintances rather than good buddies? What reward do you get from that affiliation when it is not accompanied by closeness?

5. Is it betraying your friends or your group when you try to reach out to a new group?

6. Have you ever made someone feel that she didn't belong, that you didn't want her as part of your group? What did you say and do? How did you make her feel, and how did she show her feelings? How did you feel about what you did to her?

CHAPTER 14

BELONGING: Popularity Is About Friendships

How Well Do You Get Along With Others?

Have you ever said something like, "I'd give anything to be more like Jennifer; she's so popular!" Being popular isn't really all that difficult. Those kids who are more popular, admired, or liked by others do some specific things and that's why others want to be around them. Picture in your mind a group of classmates. Who do you think are the happy people and who are the unhappy ones? Chances are you identified the students who are in groups, and who are obviously enjoying being around others, as the happy students. Probably you identified those students who are not in groups, standing alone, as the unhappy ones. Think why the people in the groups are more popular and the people standing alone are not popular.

How well you get along with others can greatly add to your self-esteem. Suppose no one in your class likes you and tomorrow you have to give an oral report. The night before The Big Day you lie in bed tossing and turning, worrying yourself sick over how you are going to do. You think because no one likes you that you will have an audience full of hostile looks or bored faces; someone might ignore you entirely, or worse, giggle or make fun of you! With all that worry going through your mind, do you really think you will do your best job on the report the next day?

Now imagine the opposite. Suppose you are a very popular student in your class and have an oral report to give the next day. Of course, you may still be slightly nervous about the report itself, but as you lie in bed that night you relax. You know that because your classmates like you, you will see them smiling at you and giving you encouraging looks. Even if you mess up a little, they will certainly cheer you on and say fun things; at the end they may even congratulate you on having done so well. You have their support and praise to look forward to. Now, how well do you think you'll give that report?

Being popular is very important to most of us. We want to have a lot of friends, enjoy good times, be part of the "in" crowd. We look at others laughing and joking and being admired, and wonder why we can't be just as popular. The good news is that anyone can be popular. All it takes is understanding a few basic rules of friendship. After all, popularity is about developing and keeping good friends.

The New Boy in Town: Roger's Story

Roger transferred into his new school at the beginning of ninth grade. He felt left out because everyone else had been friends for years. He tried very hard to become popular. He threw a couple of parties, bought little presents for people, even did the homework of the popular kids, hoping he could become part of their group. Yet, while everyone thanked him for what he did and treated him nicely, they never did anything in return to make him feel they liked him. They didn't invite him to their parties, didn't help him with hard assignments, didn't come up to sit with him in the cafeteria. He wasn't disliked or teased or anything like that, but Roger simply wasn't popular. The reason? He was constantly complaining, and criticized many students.

Gene's Story

Gene was always a loner. He never really hung around with a group of friends, never had a best friend. He considered himself happy, although he was sometimes a little wistful when other teenagers went places in groups or double-dated. Recently, John moved to the district and entered Gene's class. Because their last names were close alphabetically, the two boys sat together in a couple of classes. Soon they began working on assignments together and eventually developed a friendship. Gene noticed that as John accepted him, others did too. When Gene commented on this to John, saying that John had made him more popular, his friend laughed. "It's not me, Gene, it's you. You have become more open and willing to reach out to others. Since you and I became buddies you feel that maybe it would be fun to have other friends too. I've been watching it happen. Everyone likes you now because you like them."

Gene's self-esteem was raised by having one good friend on whom he could rely. This friendship gave him an anchor, a place where he could feel secure in being himself. Because he was himself around John and John obviously liked him, Gene began to feel good about the person he was. He felt a sense of belonging which led to a desire for more of that good feeling. As he reached out and made more friends, he found he was much happier.

As you know, being popular can make the difference between suffering through a day at school or enjoying it. Here are some key ideas to keep in mind if you want others to like and accept you (or, as you say, be more popular).

KEYS TO POPULARITY

1. Don't criticize. No one likes to be around someone who is always negative. Roger used to complain about his old school, saying how bad the teachers were. He thought he was actually complimenting the new school, talking about how good it was in comparison, but all his classmates heard was the griping. It's easy to fall into a habit of criticizing and not even know you are doing it. Listen to yourself. If you hear a lot of negativity, stop and try to rephrase things positively. How much nicer it is to hear, "Boy, this spaghetti today is really good!" than to hear, "Well, I hope this spaghetti won't poison us today like the cafeteria meat loaf did yesterday."

2. Put yourself in the other person's shoes. Before you do or say something, imagine that someone else is going to do or say that to you. How would you feel? Maybe you think you are giving constructive criticism that will really help the person, but how would you feel if he were to say that to you? You can't go wrong remembering the Golden Rule:

"Do unto others as you would have them do unto you." You'd resent a peer who acted like a teacher or a parent, telling you what to do; don't act that way to others yourself.

3. Don't be argumentative. Most things are not worth arguing about. Even if you disagree with something someone has said, how important is it to say so? Obviously, if it is something you feel strongly about, you will want to state your opinion. But in most cases, people don't want to be around others who constantly bicker and argue over ridiculous little things. If someone says a favorite singer of yours put out a dozen albums and you know she put out 16, why bring it up? All most arguments do is make the other person feel stupid and silly. Roger once found himself arguing over whether the grass on the workout field was mowed once or twice a week. He got into a shouting match with some boys over that trivial matter and made one of them feel stupid when he said, "I can't believe you're out there every day and didn't notice how often it's mowed." Of course, that boy avoided Roger from then on. The key to being popular is making others feel good about themselves.

4. Show others you accept them. Just as you want to be accepted, others want to feel part of the group. It doesn't take much to show acceptance, giving someone an invitation to a party, moving over to make an extra seat at the lunch table, including someone in a discussion. If someone feels that you don't like him, he's not going to like you. Something as simple as a smile can show acceptance.

5. Give praise and recognition. Is there anything worse than doing something special and not having it noticed? We all need to feel recognized and appreciated. Find something your classmates do well and compliment them on it. Just remember that they can see through fake praise as easily as you can. If you say something that sounds gushy, it's not going to make you popular. Give a specific compliment that shows you know what you're talking about. Roger made a new friend when he said, "That was a good science report you did, Dave. I thought I knew a lot about dinosaurs but your story about their eating habits was news to me!"

6. Don't send out what you don't want back! Life is like a boomerang. Whatever you send out there eventually finds its way back to you. If you project an image of happiness and fun, happiness and fun will come back to you. If, on the other hand, you are grumpy and depressed, always whining about how boring life is, you will soon find yourself even more depressed. You get what you give. If you give others the good, happy, cheerful, caring side of yourself, they will give you the same part of themselves.

WHAT IT TAKES TO BE A FRIEND

Being popular means working at friendship, understanding what it is all about. The following are some of the most important aspects of friendship.

Respect. Friends respect one another. They truly appreciate others' strong points and show tolerance for their weak points. Even when they completely disagree on something, they can remain close. They have a strong foundation that can accept and get past the occasional argument.

Trust. Friends have a lot of trust in each other. They know they can count on each other not to let the other one down. They make commitments and honor them, even if doing so is very difficult or inconvenient. They don't break appointments because "something better came along."

Loyalty. Friends are loyal to their friends, defending them when someone puts them down behind their backs. They are there to talk about the good things their friends do, to sing their praises. They will hang in there when friends are going through a rough time with school or parents or with problems.

Understanding. Friends make an effort to understand each other. They talk about their feelings, open up, find out what is important to each other.

Acceptance. Friends accept each other as they are. They don't try to change each other constantly, but go along with each other's little foibles and idiosyncrasies.

Communication. Friends confide in each other. They share feelings. Sometimes friends know things about each other that even parents and other family members don't know. They open up and talk about everything, big and little.

Enjoyment. Let's not forget, friends have fun with each other. They enjoy each other's company and let that enjoyment show. They often talk about how much fun they have and enjoy reminiscing about the good times they've had.

The more you understand about friendship the better friend you will be and the more popular you will become. By learning about how people think, by recognizing what you can do to make others feel good about themselves, you develop skills that help you deal well with others of all ages, backgrounds, and personality types. You become good at being popular.

TO DO . . .

1. List several people in your school who seem to be very popular. What special things do they do that make them stand out from the other students? Have they done anything special for you personally that makes you like them a lot?

_____

_____

_____

_____

2. Describe a time when you felt very popular. When and where were you? What had you done that made you feel popular? How were people treating you? Had you done something intentionally, or did it just happen?

_____
_____
_____
_____

3. Think about what makes rock stars and movie and television stars popular. Why do some singers make it and others don't when they are all talented? Why do some people just seem to be liked more than others? Do the same rules of popularity that apply to you apply to television stars and other celebrities?

_____
_____
_____
_____

4. List some of the cliques or groups you belong to. These can be in school, in sports, in clubs, at church, or in the neighborhood. How did you join that group? How do you feel about being a member? How do you show your affiliation (such as dressing alike)?

_____
_____
_____
_____

5. Describe a person in your school who belongs to several groups. Then describe a person who is very selective, who has only one best friend or is in only one tightly knit clique. What is the difference in their personalities? How do you feel about the two? Which one would you be more likely to spend time with or to help if she had a problem?

_____
_____
_____
_____

6. Define what popularity means to you. Does everyone in the school agree on who is popular? Can you think of a time when someone unpopular became popular? What did he or she do differently?

_____

_____

_____

_____

TO THINK ABOUT...

1. Can people actually plan to become popular? Can they have an organized system to make them more popular, or is that too calculated? Does popularity just happen?

2. Can someone who has been unpopular ever become popular? How can an unpopular person start over? How hard is it to change people's opinions about you?

3. Is being popular as a fourth-grader different than being popular as a high school senior? What things are the same? What things are different? How do the rules of popularity change as you grow older? Are there different kinds of popularity for boys and girls?

UNIT VI

COMPETENCE

CHAPTER 15

COMPETENCE: Do You Feel Capable?

Be Willing to Try New Things

Competence is a sense of being capable; it's a "can do" feeling. You can manage your life, resolve problems, remove obstacles, and if need be, call on others to assist when your life gets too complicated.

Being capable is an empowering feeling and increases your willingness to try new things. When you feel capable, you are willing to go that extra mile. Feeling capable actually contributes to how well you will perform and achieve. If you have an attitude of "I can do it!" chances are you can. Positive experiences build your self-image as a competent, capable person. As the saying goes, "Success breeds success." Each success stimulates further efforts, and soon you have a storehouse of positive reminders that you are capable. You feel like a winner! You behave like one, and you become one!

How Self-Esteem Affects Your Performance

Confidence provides a set of mental attitude that prepares you to respond with expectations of doing well. Look at the many positive characteristics of feeling capable. If you feel capable, you are likely to:

- be eager to try new things
- accept challenges
- self-correct when you've made mistakes or experienced failure
- use mistakes as a learning tool
- know your strengths and lead with them
- share your opinions and ideas freely
- display good sportsmanship
- have effective coping strategies for handling defeat
- recognize accomplishments and achievements
- give yourself positive self-statements and encouragement for your successes

Compare this to someone with a poor self-concept and you'll see just the opposite. This person will magnify his weaknesses and failures. The attitude of "Why try, I'm just going to lose again anyway" begins a self-defeating pattern. The message he gives himself is, "I won't be able to do it, I can't do it." Not feeling capable, he acts helpless. He's dependent on following others, even in areas where he is competent. Because of an overriding fear of failure, he is unwilling to take risks, and he is a poor loser. He uses negative self-statements ("I'm so stupid") and discounts or discredits his achievements ("I was just lucky"). How can such traits possibly lead to feelings of inner peace and joy and to experiencing outer achievement and success?

The first thing to remember is that what you believe becomes your reality. If you believe that you can do something, most of the time you can. Athletes use these beliefs all the time to improve their performances. For example, before his extraordinary Olympic performance, Brian Boitano, the 1988 gold medalist ice skater from the USA, said, "I'm confident I'll have my best performance. I'm up for this. I know I can do it." And he did! Actually, we all do the same thing to achieve success.

Nick's Story

Nick is a fifteen-year-old boy whose two older brothers were straight A students. Up until his sophomore year Nick got mostly C's. He was usually depressed and resigned to the fact that "I'm just not a brain like my brothers. I'll never be an A student; why try?" Then a student teacher helped Nick in his biology class. She involved the class in a fascinating project that really motivated Nick. He worked hard, had a good time — and made the first A he had had since elementary school! The teacher told Nick about his good marks from the front of the room, allowing his classmates to know how well Nick had done. The praise made Nick feel great. When he showed his project to his mother, she gave him a hug and said, "I always knew you could do this. You just had to believe in yourself."

After thinking about that, Nick decided he enjoyed the feeling of success. He studied more than he used to and began getting C's and B's, and some A's. He learned to respect himself. The higher his self-esteem the higher his grades went. He began a cycle that is still going strong. Not only have his grades changed, but Nick has too. He has more confidence in himself, which makes him more outgoing, friendlier, and has helped him make more friends. As Nick puts it, "Now that I like myself more, others seem to like me more too!"

Don't Be Afraid of Making Mistakes — Here's Why

I see many young people who have experienced so little success that they're afraid of making any more mistakes. These students won't initiate friendships that appear too difficult to strive for; they don't go out for activities if they think they won't do well or take a course in school that they think will be too difficult. Many schools have a rich curriculum with excellent courses designed for students to gain access to some very exciting skills, but unless these courses are mandated many young people won't sign up for them. Thus, they never realize how rich the school's curriculum really is and are unable to become as capable as they could possibly be.

You probably see a lot of people every day who are afraid of failure. They are so eager to achieve success that they won't take any chances. They won't initiate friendships with the really popular kids, won't take hard classes, won't go out for the varsity team. How about you? Are you afraid of failure? You don't have to be. Henry Ford was right when he said, "Failure is the only opportunity to more intelligently begin again."

I like Thomas Edison's story of success vs. failure. Edison didn't create the electric light on the first try! He didn't wake up one day and say, "Today's goal is to create the electric light!" Edison failed, and failed, and failed. Finally an associate of his said, "Edison, you should give up. You've failed thousands of times." "No, I haven't failed thousands of times," Edison replied. "On the contrary, I have successfully eliminated thousands of ideas that do not work!" An important skill that leads to self-confidence and a sense of capability is knowing how to solve problems effectively.

You can acquire skills that will change helpless feelings to "can do" ones. Taking responsibility and gradually exerting more influence over your own actions helps you feel capable. You can learn to make decisions and choose what the outcome will be. A good place to start is by learning how to solve problems, to generate alternatives, and then to evaluate the consequences.

Solving Problems, Generating Alternatives, and Evaluating Consequences

Having a problem and not knowing how to remedy it can be as debilitating as it is frustrating. Finding a solution and getting out of a dilemma is made even more difficult when you aren't sure what the problem is, only that one exists. In groping for a solution you may act impulsively or make rash decisions.

Effective problem-solving is a four-step process that involves identifying the real problem, searching for sound solutions and recognizing the consequences, trying them out, then evaluating the outcome. This process begins by asking four simple questions:

1. What Is the Problem?
2. How Can I Solve It? What Are the Consequences?
3. What Is My Plan?
4. How Did I Do?

Let's start out with a simple example and then build in other skills.

1. What Is the Problem?

Dan called me "stupid" and it made me mad!

2. How Can I Solve It? What Are the Consequences?

Action: I could call him stupid back.
Consequence: He will stay angry.

Action: I could punch him.
Consequence: He might hit me back.

Action: I could tell him how angry it made me.
Consequence: He would understand my feelings.

Action: I could ignore it.
Consequence: He might continue to call me names.

3. What Is My Plan? (When will you do this?)

Action: I'm going to tell him to stop name-calling. I'll tell him tomorrow morning in first period class.

4. How Did I Do? (Evaluate outcomes)

Consequence: My plan worked great. I said it politely. I didn't get in a fight. Dan said he was sorry, that he was just having a bad day.

Here's another example, and this time you get to help out.

Fifteen-year-old Mia has invited Jessica to go skiing with her and her parents in two weeks. Jessica, also 15, has told her parents of the plans and has asked for permission to go. They say she can if she has good grades on the next report card, due out in two weeks. Jessica tells Mia yes and her parents arrange for her to accompany them on the trip. The report card comes out the day prior to the planned ski trip, and Jessica has received two failing grades. She is certain her parents will not let her go on the trip now, so she doesn't give them the report card. How can Mia's problem be solved?

1. What Is the Problem?

> Jessica has accepted an invitation to go on a ski trip, and has permission based on specific criteria. Mia and her parents are expecting Jessica to go on the trip with them and have made special arrangements and accommodations based on the fact that she will attend. Jessica does not want to break the trust with her parents by not revealing the report card, but she wants Mia to accept her. After all, Mia is the most popular girl in school and besides, she has told all her friends that she is going.

2. How Can She Solve It? What Are the Consequences?

Examine the likely outcome of proposed actions by asking a question such as, "If I do that, what would happen?" Generate as many alternatives to the problem as you can, and then assess the potential impact of each option. Your goal is to learn how a different alternative leads to a different outcome. A few examples are given to get you started.

Action: She could go along with Mia by not revealing the report to her parents until after she returns home from the ski trip.

Consequence: She will break the trust she and her parents have established.

Action: She could ask her parents for permission to go based on the promise to work harder and get better grades the next quarter.

Consequence: It could be risky; her parents might say no.

Action: She could call Mia and tell her that she has decided she doesn't want to go on the trip.

Consequence: Mia will feel offended, and the friendship will be strained.

Now generate as many other alternatives as possible:

Action:

Consequence:

Action:

Consequence:

Action:
Consequence:

3. What Is the Plan? You decide what course of action Jessica will take. Jessica should:

_____
_____

4. How Did She Do? Decide what's the likely outcome, and how she will feel as a result of your proposed solution.

_____
_____

An important part of feeling capable is being able to cope with the everyday challenges of growing up. This contributes to your feelings of high self-esteem.

TO DO . . .

1. List areas in which you feel competent. Why do you feel that way? How did you achieve that competence?

_____
_____
_____
_____

2. List areas in which you feel you are incompetent. Why do you feel that way? How do you feel when you fail? How do you feel when you succeed?

_____
_____
_____
_____

3. Describe a situation in which you felt incompetent but others encouraged you and you succeeded. What happened next?

_____
_____
_____
_____
_____

4. Describe a situation in which you saw someone who was obviously competent, but felt incompetent, do a poor job. What could you say to her to make her feel better about her abilities, even though she failed?

_____
_____
_____
_____
_____

TO THINK ABOUT...

1. When you fail at an activity, how can you practice "thought stopping," making sure you don't generalize from "Well, I sure blew it this time!" to "I'm no good at this; I'll never be any good at this. Why even bother to try?"

2. Can you make a plan to deal with a problem before it begins? What type of plan would be good? What happens if you have a plan and it still fails; does that mean you are incompetent?

3. How do your parents, friends, teachers, and classmates contribute to your feelings of competence or incompetence?

CHAPTER 16

COMPETENCE: School as Your World of Work

Feeling Capable in Your "Workplace"

Just like adults, young people go to work each day. Your world of work is school; your career is that of being a student. Your ability to manage your "work life" gives you yet another sense of how competent you are. Since you spend a large portion of your waking hours in school — approximately 15,000 hours in an educational system from kindergarten through twelfth grade — you can imagine why much of your feeling of self-esteem comes from competence in this "workplace."

High Self-Esteem Students Fare Better in School

There are a lot of pay-offs in school for having a high self-esteem, because a high self-esteem student is willing to stand up for what he considers his rights. Recently, I saw proof of this again when my daughter's friend, Debra, got a B- on a paper she turned in for her history class. Debra felt that she deserved a better grade and presented her case to the teacher. The teacher took the time to sit down with her and explain in detail exactly where he thought the paper was weak. He also listened closely to her argument. The result was that Debra got a B, a slightly higher grade, but even more importantly, she got extra attention from the teacher and felt good knowing that she had the courage to stick up for what she felt she had earned. And, now that she has presented herself to her teacher as a student who is serious about her work and concerned about her grades, she's going to win the teacher's respect, consideration, and attention on future assignments. Furthermore, the extra attention will result in greater learning and will generate another measure of success, adding once more to her positive sense of self.

It's doubtful that a student with low self-esteem would take on this challenge. She would shrug and say, "I got this grade because the teacher doesn't like me." She would feel powerless to affect any other outcome. With each downbeat experience she would become less willing to attempt standing her ground when deserving or when necessary in getting her needs met.

Notice the behavior cycles created here. A student with strong self-esteem performs actions that allow her self-esteem to be strengthened even more. A student with low self-esteem doesn't perform such actions and as a result has her self-esteem lowered even more.

School Is a Tough Career, Even for Good Students

For many students, school is an intense and frustrating experience. Indeed, some students don't endure so well; some drop out psychologically, and others drop out physically. But school needn't be such a difficult experience. You can develop skills to manage your world of work. Here are some things you can do to be competent in your workplace.

1. Get organized. You will need the appropriate "tools" to begin working. That means a quiet study area safe from interruption and equipped with a good light. You'll need a desk and a bookcase. Shop for pencils, paper, and the standard supplies you'll need in your role as a student. Set up a file and learn how to use it. Get a large month-at-a-glance wall calendar to record work assignments and school-related activities. This way you can easily notice when you need to be very focused on particular projects and assignments and when you're free to schedule social activities. Keeping track of your time also helps you feel like a "professional" doing a job.

This work area doesn't have to be large, just a space that you associate with doing homework (productivity). Not having a place to work or the tools to do it is a big reason why many young people don't want to do their homework.

2. Limit interruptions. During study time there should be no TV or stereo on, no Walkman, and no phone calls. Phone calls can be made after homework projects are done or between studying different subjects as a way to take a break. If you need to clarify an assignment by talking to a fellow student, two to three minutes is sufficient. You want uninterrupted concentration. Have you seen the Nike expression, "Just Do It!" Put your mind on your work and avoid a lot of distractions. When you stop to call a friend, your mind starts wandering on all the things going on in your relationships. Save that for after your homework is done.

3. Have a regular time for studying. Whether you decide that this time is immediately after school or after the evening meal, keep it consistent when possible. This routine helps you to do your homework consistently day after day and eliminates giving yourself excuses for not doing your work.

4. Identify your work style. You may be able to complete all your studying and homework in a single session, or you may do better if you study for twenty minutes, take a break, and then come back to it. Each person is different. The important thing is that you recognize your own style and optimum pattern for producing your best work. You can identify your work style by observing the rituals that you go through before you are ready for productive work — for example, organizing your desk and sharpening all your pencils (even those you don't use). If you're overly tired, or unwilling to get into a particular assignment, what rituals help prepare you for productive work: a good tape, a brisk walk, a ten-minute bike ride? Learn how to renew your energy and channel it to the tasks that need to be done.

5. Learn to manage your time. There never seems to be enough time outside of school to do all the things you'd like to do, to get your homework assignments done, catch up with friends, take part in extracurricular activities, spend time with your family members, and still have ample time left over for yourself. A very important step in learning to manage your time is to set up a daily or weekly "to-do" list. This list shouldn't be a long and detailed one, but should contain those things that you want to accomplish each day (or week).

After you generate the list, sort out the one or two tasks that are the most urgent (in other words, set priorities). Set a timetable and estimate the length of time necessary to perform each task. Break long-term projects down into manageable parts so you can accomplish them over a period of time (days or weeks) and not wait until the last minute to get them done. Some variation on the following planning form works for most students.

DAILY PLANNING SHEET
Today's date:
Subject area:
Assignment:
When due:
Don't forget to:

TO DO . . .

1. Suppose that you did a sloppy job on an assignment and got a C-. You thought the assignment should have been a C, but you know you are capable of B work. Describe what you would say to the teacher to get your grade raised. What would you say if he pointed out you could do B work?

_____

_____

_____

_____

2. Describe the difference between making yourself feel incompetent and truly being incompetent in an area. How do you know whether you are living up to your potential?

_____
_____
_____
_____
_____

3. Analyze your daily tasks. How many of them are truly challenging? Do they help direct you toward achieving your goals?

_____
_____
_____
_____
_____

TO THINK ABOUT...

1. Is the analogy between school and the adult work world a valid one? How would your parents feel if their days were like yours in terms of being evaluated constantly and criticized?

2. Do you ever sabotage yourself and fool yourself into thinking you are incompetent when in fact you are just too lazy to make an effort? How can you distinguish fear of inability from fear of hard work?

3. When you are failing at an activity, is it best to drop it entirely, start from scratch, or attempt to patch things up? How can you tell which is the best course of action?

UNIT VII

MISSION

CHAPTER 17

MISSION: What Makes Your Life Meaningful?

A Purpose Gives Life Zest

The sixth building block in developing a positive self-image is a sense of mission, of having a purpose. For us to be inspired, life must have meaning; and we must be inspired to make meaning of life. We each need to think about how this applies to our own lives.

With vision you have direction. Having a sense of purpose means that you have in mind specific aims or intentions of what you want to do and be. When you have discovered things that are of importance to you, you're more vibrant, optimistic, and have a zest for living. What's going on excites you — you're motivated and self-directed. Inner peace, satisfaction, harmony, and greater self-knowledge are the outcomes.

A person who feels purposeful is quite different from someone who doesn't feel that his life has meaning. Not fulfilled, a low-self-esteem person often turns to others for self-fulfillment and blames them for his plight. Because he feels powerless, he stops being accountable for his actions and for his life.

Feeling Purposeful Means Taking Responsibility

A recent Gallup Poll revealed that only 25% of all people feel an overall satisfaction with their lives! Those who did express satisfaction said they were working toward two or more goals that were important to them and they had taken full responsibility for the circumstances of their lives.

You are on your way to becoming an adult, which means you get to be in full control of your own life very soon. That sounds impressive, but it means that everything is up to you — *you* are responsible for yourself, responsible for the things you say and do and think. You're responsible for your actions. You can't blame something on an imaginary playmate, as a small child might do. *A big part of growing up and maturing is recognizing that you are responsible for yourself.* When you take responsibility for your reality, you are more likely to say:

- I think about the choices I make.
- I am responsible for my actions.
- I am responsible for the level of my work.
- I am responsible for my behavior with other people.
- I am responsible for how I communicate.
- I am responsible for knowing and living my values.
- I am responsible for my own good health.

- I hang in there when the going gets tough — I can persevere in spite of difficulties.
- I can learn.

Taking responsibility for yourself is one of the prerequisites of high self-esteem. Think of yourself as being the architect of your own life. You design the plans, draw up the blueprints, oversee the construction. You don't do all of the construction yourself. Your parents, family, teachers, and others help "build" you; obviously their influences help shape the person you are going to become. But in the final analysis, what happens is up to *you*. Others will help, but it is your plan, your dream that is built. You are responsible.

There's a relationship between the life you design and the life you get. Think of what you want. You may think your teachers should get you into college. After all, isn't that what they are getting paid to do? But as you mature you will recognize that, no, teachers are not there to get you into college. They are there to help you learn, to show you how to learn, and to encourage you in your own efforts. In the final analysis, it is up to you to get yourself into college or trade school or into a job or career.

Responsibility Isn't Always Easy (or Fun)!

Being responsible isn't always easy. If you don't do your homework, for example, you don't especially enjoy having to tell that to the teacher. Instead you may make up excuses, saying that you did the wrong assignment, or you left that notebook at home, or your mother was so impressed with your beautiful work that she insisted on taking it with her to work to show it to her friends! Come to think of it, that's a pretty good excuse . . . but of course others are unlikely to believe you.

Every time you say, "My little brother was making too much noise for me to do my homework," or "I would have done my homework, but my mother wanted us to watch TV together because her favorite show was on," you give someone else control over you. When you blame others, you give them power over you. You are in effect saying, "It was their fault; they are stronger and more powerful than I am. Poor little me just couldn't help it." When you accept responsibility, even for the negative things, you reassert your own control. You say that you are the one in charge of your own life.

You can't change the past. What has happened is over and done with. What you can control are the present and the future. You can whine and moan about the past, or you can accept responsibility for it and move on. Now you must concentrate on the future, *your* future that you control. You can best do this by setting and achieving worthwhile goals.

Setting and Achieving (Worthwhile) Goals

Developing a sense of purpose means to first determine what is the purpose. Goal setting is the key. A goal is like having a map. It helps you locate the direction you should be heading so you know where you should focus your time and energy. When you get used to working toward an identified goal, you soon establish a pattern of behaving in a certain way. For instance, if you ride a bike along a particular path to school often enough, it becomes a habit, and you can follow it without even thinking, knowing that it will lead to your destination.

When you have *worthwhile* goals, you feel purposeful; you are busy working toward something important. Having goals ensures some measure of success because you are channeling your efforts in a single direction. Best of all, success in one area often leads to success in another area.

Being in Charge of Your Life

Are you managing your life? Are you shaping the direction of your life, or are you letting others do it? Some young people feel as though they have little say in their lives, believing that parents, teachers, friends, and others have more to do with what happens to them than they themselves do. If that's true for you, too, then you are assigning a lot of responsibility for the events in your life to others. That can make you feel powerless. Feeling powerless is not a good feeling. *You can shape the events in your life and determine what you want out of life*. To do this requires meaningful goals.

Are Goals Really All That Important?

Why are goals important? Goals help you *plan* what you want to have happen in your life. If you just go along, letting life happen to you, you'll have no idea what's going to occur next. It could be something wonderful . . . but then again, it could be something that you don't want to have happen. When you can't predict what's going to happen to you, things may not turn out the way you'd like them to. You may fail to accomplish anything worthwhile. You may never get what *you* want.

To put it another way: Failing to plan is planning to fail. If you fail to study that difficult material in your history class, you may not be able to pass a test on it. Or to use a sports analogy, suppose you are going to run a mile-long race. If you don't plan by eating the right foods, getting into shape, and warming up before the race; if you just tumble out of bed that morning saying brightly, "Gee, I wonder how I am going to do in this race today!" you will do poorly and feel awful when you are through, assuming you do finish! If you don't plan a meal, for example, but just close your eyes and raid the refrigerator, you might end up having whipped cream and sardines for breakfast. If you don't plan what you are going to wear, you might get up one morning and find that your clothes are dirty, and all you have to wear is a ski parka and shorts. Those are obviously silly examples, but they do illustrate how important it is to make a plan for your life.

An interesting study was made of students at Yale a few years ago. Now students at Yale are some of the most skilled, academically gifted, motivated students around. A researcher asked whether they had specific goals. Surprisingly, only about 3% had specific, well-thought-out goals. Years later a follow-up study was done on these same students. It turned out that the 3% who had set specific goals were doing better, making more money, and living more successful and happier lives than the other 97%. Why? Because they had a focus for their intelligence and skills and they knew where they were going.

The importance of setting goals can be further illustrated in the case of two drivers. One driver has a goal, a destination. He starts off and drives straight toward that goal and in due time gets there. The other driver has no goal, no destination. He takes off . . . and goes in circles. He drives around and around and around, spinning his car's wheels, using up gas and oil, never getting anywhere. Note that it makes no difference where the two drivers start off. The same is true of you. Don't worry if you think you are not as smart or as attractive as some of your friends. If you have a goal and they don't, even though you may be starting behind them, you will finish far out in front.

Count on Obstacles Along the Way

Why isn't everyone an ace goal setter? Why don't people talk more about goals? Why don't you and your friends draw up contracts to work toward your goals, saying that you will learn a new dance before the prom, actively explore all your options for an interesting career, or get a better grade on the next exam? What are the reasons, or rather the excuses, that people use to avoid being in charge of their lives?

1. "Goals Aren't All That Important." Some people don't realize the importance of goal setting. Let's face it, you and your friends don't sit around the lunch table and say, "Gee, I think we should all set goals because they are soooo important!" The topic of goals, quite probably, has never come up. Notice how many young people feel their lives are out of their control. After all, if someone else controls your life, why bother to set goals for yourself? Of course, you are ultimately responsible for your own life. You are in charge of yourself.

2. "I Don't Know How." How many courses have you had in goal setting? Probably not too many. Some young people say the reason they don't set goals is because they just don't know how. This is like saying the reason you don't build your own bicycle from scratch, or repair a car, is because you don't know how. Sure, it would be great to be able to go down to the junk yard, pick up a few pieces, and create a bicycle for almost nothing rather than having to go to the store and spend $200 or more for that same bicycle. But if you don't know how to put together a bike, you have to pay the price for not knowing. The same is true with goals. If you don't know how to create or set a goal, you pay the price. The good news is that goal setting is not difficult.

3. "What if Someone Makes Fun of My Goal?" A third reason some people don't set goals is because they fear being criticized. Suppose your goal is to lose 10 pounds by the end of the year. When you tell your best friend, she says, "Oh, that's impossible. You can't do that. You're always trying to lose weight and you never do." Or maybe your goal is to be a starter on the basketball team. You tell your friend who immediately snickers and says, "That team doesn't want you. It wants someone tall, with fast hands, and the ability to block. You're just wasting your time!"

Unfortunately, your friends, whether for a good reason or out of jealousy, often will ridicule your goals. Maybe those friends are concerned that if you achieve your goal you will be more popular and not want to be around them anymore. Maybe those friends sincerely want to help and are trying, in their opinion, to keep you from making a mistake or making a fool of yourself. Whatever the reason, people often criticize other people's goals. The solution is to share goals only with those who are supportive of you. Otherwise, keep your goals to yourself! This is especially true if your goal is a big one, like being the star player on the team when you are now second string, or losing 30 pounds when you have never dieted successfully before. You can't be criticized by others for something they know nothing about.

4. "I Might Fail!" Another reason that some people don't set goals is the fear of failure. So what if you do fail? Suppose you get a B on an exam instead of an A. Is that a failure? No, you have learned most of the material and now know that you need to study even harder the next time. From every mistake you learn something. From every disappointment you become stronger. If you let the fear of failure prevent you from setting goals, you are losing the power to shape your own life, to make it what you want it to be.

By learning how to formulate purposeful goals, you feel good about yourself, proud and confident. That's the whole idea. In order to succeed at your goals, you have to make certain that they are realistic and obtainable. There are seven steps that set the pattern for becoming a successful goal setter.

SEVEN STEPS TO GOAL SETTING

1. Desire a challenging goal. You have to be determined to get what you want. If you don't really want the goal, it's unlikely you will make the commitment to accomplish it, and you'll give up when faced with hard work. There's a saying that goes, "Most people don't aim too high and miss, they aim too low and hit!" The same will be true for you if you set goals that are too easy. If your goal is to get at least a C on your paper and you know you can do better, what's the challenge? If your goal is to do at least 25 sit-ups and you are already able to do 23 with no problem at all, what's the challenge?

2. Own the goal. Your goal must be your own. It has to be one that you yourself want. When someone else sets goals for you, you're not going to be very motivated toward achieving them. If your parents want you to be a good student, that's one thing. But if you want to be a good student, that's another. You are likely to be a good student because that is your goal, too. You must have an inner voice, a drive that says, "This is important to me."

3. Believe you can achieve your goal. You have to believe that you can meet your goal. Therefore, it must be achievable — not necessarily easy, but there has to be a better than 50-50 chance you can meet the goal. You don't want a goal that is self-defeating, one that is so hard you almost certainly will not achieve it. Set a goal that you personally can achieve. If you set a goal of learning to fix your car, but only read a few books on the subject because you don't really think you are a good enough mechanic to do the job, it is going to take you forever to learn anything. On the other hand, if you sincerely believe in your goal and feel that you can learn to work on your car, that you can become a skilled mechanic, you're going to take a class, talk to other mechanics, and read those books. You are going to accomplish your goal a lot more quickly.

4. Put your goals in writing. Writing down your goals clarifies them in your mind. Writing down goals also keeps you organized and helps you internalize or "buy into" your commitment. If you just think about your goal, you can forget about it just as easily. We have hundreds of thousands of thoughts daily and most of these are forgotten in moments. But the ones we take the time and effort to write down seem to matter more. Suppose that you want to build a house and you hire an architect. He meets with you and says, "I have a lot of great ideas. Here I am going to put the master bedroom with high ceilings; here I am going to put the jacuzzi; here I am going to put the swimming pool . . ." You listen for a while, then say, "I am having trouble remembering and visualizing all this. May I see your blueprints please?" The architect smiles at you and says, "Blueprints? I never write anything down. I keep it all in my head!" Ha! Are you going to let that person build your house, or are you going to get someone who has a plan he can put down on paper? Even if the architect is a genius, no one can work without a blueprint. The same is true for you and your goals. Writing them down gives you a blueprint to direct your efforts.

5. Think about the benefits of achieving your goal. What are the benefits of achieving your goal? What makes it worth the effort of accomplishing? For example, suppose you want to get in shape. How many benefits can you think of? You will look better, maybe get more attention and more dates. You will feel better physically, maybe get stronger and do better in sports. You will feel better emotionally, have more confidence and self-esteem. The more reasons you have for achieving the goal the stronger will be your desire, and the stronger the desire the easier it is to reach your goal.

6. Set a deadline or date for completing your goal. You want to have a definite commitment to an ending point. Is your goal a long-term one, such as getting into a good college? Or is it a short-term one, such as doing well on the exam next Tuesday? In many cases, the very best kind are long-term goals broken down into short-term goals. For example, getting into college is the long-term goal, an overall dream. But in order to reach that long-term goal, you need many short-term goals, ranging from doing well in each of your classes to getting the money together for tuition. Goals and deadlines seem much easier to reach when they are broken down into manageable tasks.

Have dates for everything, major and minor. Some dates are set for you. If you are going to take the SAT college admission exam, for example, you know that you have to be prepared and have all your studying done by the date of the exam. In addition, set intermediate deadlines: have the vocabulary learned by this date, the math by that date. Having a date written down motivates you. It also helps you prioritize where and how you will allocate (spend) your time. Then, if you know the deadline is near, you can push yourself just a little harder. When you do accomplish your goal within the deadline, you feel like a winner.

A word of caution: Don't set overly ambitious deadlines. Don't say you are going to make 10 new friends this month if you're a very shy person who has trouble making five new friends a year. Don't say that by the end of this semester you are going to take 10 seconds off your sprint time if you have not taken off more than one second a semester so far. Set a realistic deadline. You can do just about anything you set your mind to as long as you give yourself sufficient time to do so. You can get an A on your Spanish exam if you take the time to study for it. You can clear up your complexion in six weeks if you practice good hygiene.

7. Set a reward for the completion of your goal. Let's say that you have gone through all the six steps. You have set a goal and accomplished it. Now reward yourself! You did something you set your mind to do, and you deserve to be proud of yourself. What one nice thing will you do for yourself because you have been diligent and hard at work on your goal? Maybe it's a few days of "downtime," or a new item of clothing, or tickets to a special concert.

TO DO...

1. Describe how you feel about yourself and your life right now. Are you in control, or are you just letting things happen?

_____
_____
_____
_____
_____

2. Think of a time when you had a goal and a plan, and worked toward that goal in an organized manner. Did you succeed on the first try? Explain.

_____
_____
_____
_____
_____

3. Did you ever feel like giving up? If so, when?

_____
_____
_____
_____
_____

4. List two areas of your life in which you feel you have control and confidence.

_____
_____
_____
_____
_____

5. What are two areas of your life that you let operate by "accident"?

_____
_____
_____
_____
_____

TO THINK ABOUT...

1. What goals have your family members or friends set and achieved? How did they feel afterward?

2. Can you identify the goals of your successful classmates? Are they the same as or different than yours?

3. Think of areas in your life where you'd like to have more control. How can you take charge there?

CHAPTER 18

MISSION: Setting Goals Is the Key

Life Is a Do-It-Yourself Project

In the previous chapter you learned that having goals is one way of making life purposeful and that a purpose or mission in life can enhance self-esteem. In this chapter I'll go into more detail on how to set goals. Remember, life really is a do-it-yourself project. Your parents, teachers, and friends may be able to help you make your life better, but in the final analysis it's all up to you. Now it's time to match your strengths with your dreams and to set goals that are meaningful to you. Here's how.

Focus on Your Area of Excellence

Everyone has something at which he or she excels. You might be good at acting, while your best friend is a strong athlete, and another friend finds math and science easy. Sometimes it takes a while to find those areas of excellence, but they are there. Why do you think you go to school and study so many different subjects? Not everyone is going to use the skills he or she learns in biology class in the future, but everyone still has to be exposed to this class. Why? One reason is so everyone can find his or her area of expertise. The more things you are exposed to, the better your chances of finding what you are really good at. If you read the biographies of successful people, you will often find that there was one turning point in each person's life. For example, a dancer might have been taken to the ballet by her parents when she was just a child and said, "That's it, that's what I want to do with my life." Or an actor might have taken an easy class in drama just to get the credit. Then he discovered he had a talent for acting and later became a star. These individuals achieved success because they discovered what they had an interest in.

How Can You Tell What You Are Good at?

In what areas should you set your goals? One key is discovering what captures your attention. You do better in those things that interest you and worse in those that don't hold your interest. In a physical education class you might be good at volleyball because you like it. But how good are you at square dancing? If you don't want to dance, you might do so anyway because the teacher makes you, but you won't try very hard. And of course, if you want to be successful, you have to try very hard.

Have you ever been doing something and lost all track of time? Have you ever been involved in a project and suddenly found that several hours had passed and you hadn't even realized it? We've all had that experience. Watch for the times when you are so absorbed or involved in a project that nothing else seems to matter. You are concentrating on that project because it interests you. That means that you are probably good in this area, or can become good in it.

NOTE: This does not mean you should stop working in subjects that are not your best. If you find history difficult, you still have to study for the tests and pass the class. I'm not suggesting that you say, "I never do well in this, so I may as well not waste any more time on it." That would be a great way for students to get out of learning algebra or biology, but you need to put effort into all areas. What I am saying, however, is that there will be one (or perhaps more than one) area in which you excel. Put *extra* time and effort into that area.

Finding Your Acres of Diamonds

Another key to goal setting is contained in the Acres of Diamonds concept. A friend of mine illustrates this concept by telling the story about a farmer who got bored with farming and decided to seek his fortune in a gold mine. After selling his farm, he moved to Alaska to search for gold. He was gone many years and had all sorts of adventures, but he never did find gold. He lived a very poor life, sometimes not having enough food, and never having a nice place to live. Finally, exhausted and out of hope, he traveled back to see his former farm, just for old times' sake. To his amazement he found that a mansion stood where the farmhouse had been and the grounds were gorgeous. The new owner came out to talk to the former farmer. "What on earth happened here?" asked the bewildered farmer. "You barely had enough money to buy the farm from me, as I remember. How did you get so rich?"

The new owner just smiled. "Actually, it was all due to you. There were diamonds on this property — acres and acres of diamonds!"

The old farmer scoffed. "Diamonds! I knew every inch of this land and there were no diamonds here."

The new owner nodded and pulled from his pocket a lump of what looked like coal. "I carry around this small one as a good luck charm. Here is one of the diamonds from this property."

The farmer was amazed. "That's a diamond? I remember seeing a lot of those all over this land. I used to swear at them and kick them because they got in the way when I was plowing. I thought they were lumps of coal! That doesn't look anything like a diamond to me!"

The farmer didn't recognize the diamonds when he saw them. Not all diamonds look like diamonds; in their unpolished form they may look like lumps of coal. You have diamonds in your life right now that you may not be recognizing. Something that seems worthless or silly may, with some polishing, be extremely valuable. For example, an ability to mimic people may be more than just a fun thing to do at parties — maybe it's a sign that you have dramatic ability and could be a good actor, with practice. If you are able to explain things to your classmates so that they are always asking you for help, you might think that you have a skill that is a pain in the neck since others pester you a lot. However, with practice, that skill could make you a good teacher, professor, consultant, or public speaker. The point is to know that you have those diamonds. First you must find them, then you can polish them so they look like the diamonds they really are.

EXERCISE 1: Identifying Your Acres of Diamonds

1. What subjects capture your attention? When you're looking for a book in the library, what do you pick up and read? What informational programs do you watch on television? What classes do you really enjoy? List them below.

_____
_____
_____

2. What activities do you most enjoy doing?

_____
_____
_____

3. When do you feel completely absorbed in what you are doing?

_____
_____
_____

EXERCISE 2: Finding Your Area of Excellence

1. List skills you have in each area below. These skills can be major or relatively minor. The goal of this exercise is to make you think of all the many talents you really do have.

Academic _____

Social _____

Family _____

Athletic _____

Artistic _____

Literary _____

Dramatic _____

Other _____

2. Which of these skills do you consider your own personal "diamonds"?

_____

_____

EXERCISE 3. Determining Your Number One Goal

We are most likely to have a purposeful life when our goals are in balance. There are nine areas that give our life balance. Write two goals in each of these areas.

1. Spiritual growth: Goals for peace of mind, search for meaning, spiritual fulfillment.

_____

_____

2. Personal relationships: Goals in your relationships (with parents, friends, teachers, others).

_____

_____

3. Learning/education: What would you like to know more about? What skills do you want to develop?

_____

_____

4. Status and respect: To which groups do you want to belong? From whom do you want respect?

_____

_____

5. Leisure time: What activities (hobbies, sports, vacations) would you like to learn more about? To do more of?

6. Fitness: Goals for your physical fitness and overall health.

_____

_____

7. Financial: Goals for having enough money to do what you want to do.

_____

_____

8. Job/career: What kind of job would you like? What are your goals for productive work and career success?

_____

_____

9. Others: Goals that may not fit into the previous categories.

_____

_____

EXERCISE 4: Setting Subgoals

Some goals will take a while to accomplish. These you will need to break down into manageable parts. Breaking a goal into subgoals can help you know where to begin and determine what to do when. Here's an example.

MAJOR GOAL: Go to college.

SUBGOALS

June: Take a tutoring course to prepare for the SAT.

July: Take the SAT.

September: Gather letters of recommendation; research college choices.

October: Pick five colleges and get application forms.

November: Complete and mail college applications.

December: Apply for financial aid, etc.

Choose one of your goals and complete the following steps.

Goal:_____

_____

Subgoals:_____

_____

_____

_____

OVERCOMING OBSTACLES/REMOVING THE BARRIERS

Now you'll want to remove all of the reasons that prevent you from realizing the goals you want to achieve. You'll want to overcome the obstacles and remove the barriers. Here are the steps.

1. Identify the obstacles. If your goal is to be allowed to go on an overnight camping trip with your friends, the major obstacle might be that your mother has said you cannot go. A second obstacle might be that you don't have the money for the trip. And a third obstacle might be that you have to spend that weekend studying for a final exam in history. These odds might look overwhelming, but don't be discouraged! All goals have obstacles. The more obstacles you can identify, the easier it will be once you start to work toward accomplishing your goal.

2. Identify the knowledge you require. Once you have set the goals and identified the obstacles, the next step is to find out what you need to know to overcome the obstacles. Think of this in terms of school. If you want to do well on a Spanish test, you have to iden-tify what material is on the test so you can study it. If the test is going to include irregular verbs or the preterit, you need to know this in order to study. If you don't know what is on the exam, you might study all the wrong material. Even though your general knowledge is improved, that will be small comfort when you get back your exam with a D on it. When you've identified the gaps in your knowledge, rank them in priority before filling them in. For example, before you begin driving, you may not know about road etiquette (manners among drivers) nor about safety rules. Which is more important to know? Obviously, the safety rules. Find out what knowledge you need, then decide in which order you are going to acquire that knowledge.

3. Identify the people who can help. The third step is to find out who can help you meet your goals. Suppose your goal is to get an athletic scholarship to college. The coach can help you meet that goal. You don't have to do everything by yourself. In fact most of us feel terrific when we are able to help someone else. People are usually eager to do what they can to help you. When you run up against an obstacle, when you are setting a goal that seems hard to accomplish, identify your personal resources. Whom do you know who can help you?

4. Make a plan. You need to have a plan before you begin taking action, otherwise you will waste a lot of time and become frustrated. Remember that architect who had no blueprint? He might start building without having the materials, without knowing what he's working on, then end up with a chicken coop when he was supposed to build a doghouse. If you don't have a plan, you can make all sorts of mistakes. A plan is really a list of activities. Decide what you need to do. Try to think of every single step. Be as specific as possible. For example, you want to win the science fair with your project. What activities can you undertake toward accomplishing that goal? Don't just say, "Build the best project." That's too vague. Be more specific. You can get several books on the subject. You can talk to others who have built projects like yours so that you know what problems they had and how they overcame them. You can begin gathering the materials you will need. You can get a commitment from your science teacher to spend time with you reviewing the project.

You can put together the actual project, then begin the paperwork. You can ask your older brother to type your report. When you first begin learning this planning skill, you may find that you can't think of very many things to write down in your plan. But as you get better and better, your plan will become more complete. And the more complete the plan, the easier it is to reach your goal. Once you have your list of activities, the next step is to *prioritize* them. Assign them levels of importance. Doing so lets you know where to begin your efforts.

5. Visualize. When you visualize something, you see it in your mind. You create a mental picture of yourself doing what you want to do. The subconscious does only what you tell it to do. If you consciously think of something, the subconscious will kick into gear and get busy doing the work you want it to do. Have you ever heard the expression, "What you see is what you get?" That summarizes visualization very well. If you see yourself working toward your goals and ultimately achieving them, that's exactly what will happen.

6. Be determined and persistent. If something is worth doing, if it's a goal, most likely it will not be all that easy to achieve. It takes determination to meet your goals, and persistence to hang in there when things are rough. You can do whatever you set your mind to do. Anticipate the difficulties, and never give up.

TO DO . . .

EXERCISE 1: Accomplishing Your Goal

Think of a goal you would like to accomplish but that appears too difficult to obtain now. Choose one that seems to have a lot of obstacles in the way. Then go through these six steps and try to see how you could accomplish that goal. Let's use Martin's goal.

Martin's Goal: "I want to be a starter on the basketball team."

Obstacles: All the starting positions are already filled. Even though I'm the best second-stringer on the team, I may not be able to improve enough to take over a starting position, especially if all the starters improve, too.

Needed knowledge: I need to know what the coach is looking for in starters. I need to know the most important thing for me to work on improving.

People who can help: The coach can tell me what he values most in a player. My friends can help by playing basketball with me when we get together, instead of watching movies. My parents can help me watch what I eat and be understanding about my needing more free time for practice.

My plan: I need to make a workout schedule and stick to it. I need to get people involved in helping me reach my goal.

Visualization: I will see the crowd cheer as I make a block or score a basket.

Determination and persistence: I won't get discouraged. I'll concentrate on being the best player I can be.

Now you try it.

Goal: _____

_____

Identify the obstacles: _____

_____

Identify the knowledge you require: _____

_____

Identify the people who can help: _____

_____

Make a plan: _____

_____

Visualize: _____

_____

Be determined and persistent: _____

_____

TO THINK ABOUT...

1. How do you know whom to ask for help? And what do you do if someone refuses to help you, maybe out of jealousy or fear that you will improve too much?

2. Think of things you can do to keep from getting too discouraged if you lose your commitment and get away from your goals for a little while.

3. What do you think is the biggest obstacle to achieving your goals?

CHAPTER 19

MISSION: Putting It All Together

Living Life With a Purpose

Throughout this book you have been studying the importance of a healthy self-esteem and the elements needed to develop and nurture your self-esteem. In this final chapter I'd like to take a more general view. I'd like you to think about the purpose of your life, about why you are here, about what makes your life satisfying or unsatisfying, successful or unsuccessful. Like most of us, you increase your self-esteem when you feel safe, secure, happy, connected, capable, and successful. The good news is that it's easy to be all those things. You can choose how you want your life to be! Here are six keys to making your choices work.

KEYS TO SUCCESS

1. An inner calm. Inner calm is the feeling that you have done your best. When you know and understand yourself, and feel that you are doing well in your relationships, goals, work, school, job, and athletics, you have peace of mind. However, when you're doing well in school, but aren't getting along with your parents, you probably won't be in a state of inner calm. Your peace of mind will be greatest when you find balance in your life (personal, scholastic, and social). My friend Ken Blanchard says it this way, "There is no pillow so soft as a clear conscience."

2. Health and energy. Persons with high self-esteem value their health. You need to be healthy and energetic to do all the things you want to do in life. And only if you have sustained good health will you be able to enjoy the fruits of your efforts.

3. Loving relationships. Many of us think of success as having a good career, an expensive house, a fancy car, and a lot of money. Though these things certainly are nice to have, they seem relatively insignificant if your father or mother doesn't love you, or if you have very few friends. If you got an A on a project but your classmates didn't congratulate you, or if they made fun of you, how would you feel? The admiration and love of our friends and family are what's really important in life.

Individuals who have developed close friendships, strong family ties, and loving relationships have a greater sense of wholeness than do those without these ties. By demonstrating your interest in others, in their ideas and activities and feelings, you provide the basis for mutually fortifying relationships. Other people are an essential part of our lives, as this saying illustrates: "There are rubber balls and glass balls in life. The goal is to know which is which. Family, health, and friends are the glass balls. You must never drop the glass balls."

4. Financial freedom. Financial success is a worthy goal; it's perfectly okay to want and enjoy money. While it can't be the whole focus of your life, of course, earning enough money is important because of what it represents: financial freedom. Your parents, for instance, don't want to worry about where the next meal is coming from or how they're going to pay the rent. Being financially secure allows them to pay these bills without pressure.

Perhaps you know persons who have convinced themselves that acquiring masses of money and the material things money can buy signifies the achievement of success and status. They think they can gain respect by owning more things than those around them. But this isn't true. That's why so many who seek happiness through material wealth are unsatisfied. It's not money but what it can do that's important. Just having money or material possessions is not enough. Knowledge, achievement, personal satisfaction, and high self-esteem are also indicators of wealth. So you see, the value of money is relative. You need to think about money in terms of how you will go about earning enough for the life you want to build, and the goals you want to achieve in the course of your lifetime.

5. Purposeful goals. Your goals should be worthwhile to you. That may mean something different to everyone. Maybe you think that worthwhile means earning a lot of money, becoming a rabbi or a doctor, or earning a Ph.D. degree. But these goals don't have to be just career accomplishments. You do something worthwhile when you are nice to your little brother, when you are a caring son, daughter, friend, or student.

6. Personal fulfillment. When you do what you enjoy, what you feel you are meant to do, and do it well, you experience personal fulfillment. Personal fulfillment means your life is on the right track and everything seems to be running smoothly. It's that warm feeling that says you are doing your best, not necessarily *the* best, but *your* best. For example, maybe after a lot of practice you lowered your sprint time or raised your math score. Even if you're not the fastest runner on the team or the top mathematician in the class, you did your best and are happy. Ultimately, you have only one critic to satisfy and that's the hardest one: yourself. The following poem talks about the need to be honest with yourself in order to live a personally fulfilling life.

The Person Staring Back From the Glass

When you get what you want in your struggle for self,
And the world makes you king/queen for a day,
Then go to the mirror and look at yourself,
And see what that person has to say.

For it isn't your father, or mother, brother or sister
Whose judgment upon you must pass,
The person whose verdict counts most in your life
Is the one staring back from the glass.

> That's the person to please, never mind all the rest,
> For he's/she's with you clear to the end.
> And you've passed the most dangerous, difficult test,
> If the one in the glass is your friend.
>
> You can fool the whole world down the pathway of years,
> And get pats on the back as you pass,
> But your final reward will be heartaches and tears,
> If you've cheated the one in the glass.
>
> —Author Anonymous

TO DO . . .

EXERCISE 1: Defining Success for Yourself

See how you can apply these keys to your own life. Choose one person you know who appears to be successful. Now go through the six keys to success again. For each key, write an example of how it is used by the successful person you listed. An example will help you get started.

SUCCESSFUL PERSON: My brother Kevin.

Inner Calm: He rarely seems to worry and is usually cheerful. If he fails at something, he shrugs and says, "Well, I did my very best and I can't ask anything more than that of myself."

Health and Energy: An athlete, Kevin works out at the gym a couple times a week. He takes care of himself, eating right and getting enough sleep. He always seems to keep going when the rest of us are tired and ready to give up.

Loving Relationships: Kevin doesn't have a girlfriend right now, but he has a lot of good friends and he always seems to be involved in fun activities. He is close to me and the rest of our family.

Financial Freedom: From his part-time job at a fast-food place Kevin makes enough money to enjoy his friends and to take care of his car. He is putting a little money away for college. Although he doesn't have as much money as he'd like and has to be careful about saving, he's never broke.

Purposeful Goals: Kevin wants to get a good job after college and make enough money to send our parents to Hawaii for their twenty-fifth wedding anniversary. He also wants to get involved in politics and maybe even run for office to do what he can to improve the community.

Personal Fulfillment: Kevin likes himself. He is comfortable being himself.

Now you try it.

SUCCESSFUL PERSON: _____

Inner Calm: _____
_____

Health and Energy: _____
_____

Loving Relationships: _____
_____

Financial Freedom: _____
_____

Purposeful Goals: _____
_____

Personal Fulfillment: _____
_____

EXERCISE 2: Goals for Your Success

What steps can you take toward using each key in your own life? An example is given to help you get started.

Inner Calm: I will keep assuring myself that I am doing my best; I will give myself a break and not expect perfection. The next time I make a mistake I will forgive myself.

Health and Energy: I will start eating the right foods, cutting back on junk foods. I will get more exercise and enough sleep.

Loving Relationships: I will spend more time with my family and show them how much I care about them. I will think about my friends' feelings more and let them know I'm glad we're friends. When I'm depressed I will not hesitate to let my family and friends help me.

Financial Freedom: I will keep track of where my money goes, marking down what I spend it on. Then I will analyze that list and resolve to stop wasting money. I will try to save a little of my allowance or the paycheck from my part-time job so that there will always be a little money in the bank in case I want something special.

Purposeful Goals: I will think of what I can do to make life better for my family and friends and for everyone around me. I will try to do at least one nice thing for someone else every time I do one nice thing for myself.

Personal Fulfillment: I will count my blessings! I will note how lucky I am to be healthy and loved and to have friends. I will think about how terrific my life is and how many good things there are about being me.

Now you try it.

Peace of Mind: _____

_____

Health and Energy: _____

_____

Loving Relationships: _____

_____

Financial Freedom: _____

_____

Purposeful Goals : _____

_____

Personal Fulfillment: _____

_____

TO THINK ABOUT...

1. As you grow older, does your purpose or your sense of mission in life change? What were your goals when you were little and how did accomplishing them lead you to become the person you are today?

2. Do you think about your goals and purposes on a daily basis, or do you create grand goals and think about them only once in a while? How can you keep track of your progress toward accomplishing your mission? Do you reward yourself for making progress?

3. Should you share your sense of mission with your friends and family and teachers? What if they make fun of you? Is a mission easier to accomplish if you keep it to yourself, or should you try to get help along the way from others?

IT BEGINS WITH YOU: A Message From the Author

Liking Yourself Is the Key to Liking Others

It all begins with you. Have you ever noticed how some of the grumpiest and most bitter people are the ones who actually don't like themselves very well? Think about how this relates to your own life. When you feel bad about yourself, when you think you are doing poorly in school or you have been rude to your friends or parents, you don't like other people either. It is human nature to say, "That looks awful on you," or "What a nerd!" when in fact you are thinking, "I don't feel so good about myself today." If you want others to care about *you*, then you first must learn to care about and love yourself. You have to like yourself. You have to *value* yourself. Here are some key elements:

1. Accept yourself. No one is perfect — not even the most gorgeous or handsome celebrity or the most brilliant scientist. No one can be everything. Recognize that you are not perfect and say, "Well, that's okay. I still like myself." Of course, accepting yourself does not mean you stop trying to improve. You know that many, many things *are* in your control, that you can take charge of your own life. Be honest and motivated. Say, "I accept the fact that I am not as intelligent as some of my friends. But I work hard and do the best I can, and I like that about myself. I am going to keep working hard and try to do my best all the time."

2. Be responsible. Practice *self-responsibility*. You are responsible for yourself, for your thoughts. You are no longer dependent on everyone else to tell you what to think. You can't give control of your life over to someone else. Once you accept responsibility you'll appreciate yourself more, and like yourself better. No one wants to feel helpless. Feeling in control provides you with a positive sense of self-power.

3. Forgive yourself. *Forgive yourself when you make mistakes*. You'll always be changing, learning new things. Only through trying new things can we grow and mature. After all, you could keep taking math tests where you add 2+2 and never make a mistake . . . but how much fun would that be, and how much would you like and respect yourself? So you take algebra instead and get frustrated because you make a lot of mistakes. Forgive yourself! Don't hold a grudge against yourself. Many people do just that, living in the past and fretting about something stupid they did. When you dwell on a mistake, like thinking about the time you told your best friend's secret and betrayed his trust, you feel awful about yourself. Take steps to remedy the situation, like apologizing sincerely to your friend, and then forgive yourself. It's time to move on.

4. Set purposeful and worthwhile goals. There's nothing wrong with being an idealist. Go ahead and set the goal of helping to improve the world. In some way you can do just that. Maybe you will make the world better by training for a career that helps others or by helping keep world peace. Maybe you will make the world better by rearing wonderful children. Maybe you will make the world better just by being you, someone happy and kind to others. If you set a good goal, a great and worthwhile goal, you will begin to think that you are a pretty special, giving, loving person — and what's not to like about someone like that?

5. Respect yourself. You gain respect by first respecting yourself. Live up to your word. Identify your values and watch your actions because these show what your values are. Do what you believe in. Respect and stand up for your principles. You will be challenged to defend your values, something you believe in. You may lose some of your friends or be unpopular with a certain crowd when you protect your values. But think about it. How do you feel about your friends when they stand up for their beliefs? More often than not you admire their courage. You don't necessarily need to agree with a person to respect and like him. But when you love and respect yourself, you will find it easier to love and respect those around you.

6. Follow the golden rule. Treat other people the way you want them to treat you. This principle is the foundation of all else. If you want to be treated with respect, respect others. If you want to be smiled at, smile at others. If you want to be welcome in a group, be certain you welcome others to your group. Sometimes it happens that you are nice to a person and he is mean back. You have little control over others, only over yourself. If you treat others kindly no matter how they treat you, you will be proud of yourself and like yourself more. The Golden Rule is powerful. It has been the foundation of whole religions and civilizations and almost every successful person's self-esteem.

7. Share your love. When you like yourself and love yourself, then you are ready to share your love with others. Love grows by sharing it. You can practice telling people how you feel about them, starting with your parents. You might think it's corny to say, "I love you, Dad." You might come from a family that doesn't talk much about love. So you be the first! Your parents want and need your love and respect just as much as you want and need theirs.

You can show your love in hundreds of little ways, from being sympathetic and listening to stories of their hard days to doing something nice like extra chores. You can also verbalize your love. Start by ending a conversation with, "Love you, Mom (or Dad)." When you are talking, you can toss in a casual, "You know, I really love you, and I'm so glad you're my parents." What they hear is, "I love you. I appreciate the things you do for me. You mean everything to me." Say it so your parents *know* it.

You can share your love with others as well. Don't confuse being *in* love with having a loving relationship. You don't have to be *in* love with someone; that may come later. Yet aren't there people you do love, like your best friend? Love comes in many forms. You don't have to be romantically, passionately, head-over-heels in love with someone to have a loving relationship. A special look between you and a friend, a touch on the arm — all these things show your care, affection, and love.

8. Make a difference in the world. Think about how you can contribute to the world, and do something for others. You can make a difference. Let the world know that you were here by making the world better for having had you in it. Develop loving relationships, first by loving yourself, and then by sharing your love with others. Love creates the energy and synergy that universally binds us all. Let your lifework — that career or job that you want to do for a living — reflect these values.

As you follow these steps, you grow to appreciate the wonderful person you are.

I wish you the best — in school — and in your life.

— Bettie B. Youngs

Resources and Suggested Readings

Ackoff, R. *The Art of Problem Solving*. New York: John Wiley and Sons, 1978.

Anderson, E., G. Tedman, and C. Rogers. *Self-Esteem for Tots to Teens*. New York: Meadowbrook/Simon and Schuster, 1984.

Anglund, J. W. *A Friend Is Someone Who Likes You*. New York: Hartcourt and Brace, 1985.

Axline, V. M. *Dibs: In Search of Self*. New York: Ballantine Books, 1967.

Barksdale, L. S. *Essays on Self-Esteem*. Idyllwild, CA: The Barksdale Foundation, 1977.

Baron, J. D. *Kids and Drugs*. New York: Putnam, 1983.

Beane, J., and R. Lipka. *Self Concept, Self-Esteem and the Curriculum*. New York: Teachers College Press, 1984.

Bedley, G. *The ABCD's of Discipline*. Irvine, CA: People-Wise Publications, 1979.

Bennett, W. *Schools Without Drugs*. U.S. Department of Education: White House, Washington, D.C. 1989.

Bergstrom, C. *Losing Your Best Friend: Losing Friendship*. New York: Human Science Press, 1984.

Berne, E. *What Do You Say After You Say Hello?* New York: Grove Press, 1971.

Berne, P., and L. Savary. *Building Self-Esteem in Children*. New York: Continuum, 1989.

Bessell, H., and T. Kelly, Jr. *The Parent Book*. Rolling Hills Estates, CA: Jalmar Press, 1977.

Betancourt, J. *Am I Normal?* New York: Avon, 1983.

Bingham, E. E., and S. J. Stryker. *CHOICES: A Teen Man's Journal for Self-Awareness and Personal Planning*. El Toro, CA: Mission Publications, 1985.

Bingham, E. E., and S. J. Stryker. *CHOICES: A Teen Woman's Journal for Self-Awareness and Personal Planning*. El Toro, CA: Mission Publications, 1985.

Blume, J. *Are You There, God? It's Me, Margaret*. New York: Dell, 1970.

Blume, J. *Then Again, Maybe I Won't*. New York: Dell, 1971.

Bonny, H., and L. Savary. *Music and Your Mind*. New York: Harper & Row, 1973.

Borba, M. *Esteem Builders*. Rolling Hills Estates, CA: Jalmar Press, 1989.

Bradley, B. *Where Do I Belong? A Kid's Guide to Stepfamilies*. Reading, MA: Addison-Wesley, 1982.

Branden, N. *Psychology of Self-Esteem*. Los Angeles: Bantam Books, Nash Publishing Co., 1969.

Branden, N. "What is Self-Esteem?" First International Conference on Self-Esteem: August 1990, Asker, Norway. Paper presented.

Briggs, D. C. *Celebrate Yourself*. Garden City, NY: Doubleday, 1977.

Briggs, D. C. *Your Child's Self-Esteem*. New York: Dolphin Books, Doubleday & Company, 1975.

Brookover, W. B. *Self-Concept of Ability and School Achievement.* East Lansing, MI: Office of Research and Public Information, Michigan State University, 1965.

Buntman, P. H. *How to Live With Your Teenager.* New York: Ballantine Books, 1979.

Buscaglia, L. *Living, Loving & Learning.* Thorofare, NJ: Charles B. Slack, 1982.

Buscaglia, L. *Love.* Thorofare, NJ: Charles B. Slack, 1972.

"Children Having Children: Teen Pregnancy in America." *TIME.* December 9, 1985, pp. 78-90.

Clems, H., and R. Bean. *Self-Esteem: The Key to Your Child's Well-Being.* New York: Putnam, 1981.

Coopersmith, S. *The Antecedents of Self-Esteem.* San Francisco, CA: W. H. Freeman, 1967.

Covington, M. "Self-Esteem and Failure in School." *The Social Importance of Self-Esteem.* University of California Press, Berkeley, CA, 1989.

Crockenberg, S., and B. Soby. "Self-Esteem and Teenage Pregnancy," *The Social Importance of Self-Esteem.* University of California Press, Berkeley, CA, 1989.

Crow, L., and A. Crow. *How to Study.* New York: Collier Books, 1980.

Curran, D. *Traits of a Healthy Family.* Minneapolis, MN: Winston, 1983.

Danziger, P. *The Cat Ate My Gymsuit.* New York: Dell, 1973.

Davis, L., and J. Davis. *How to Live Almost Happily with Your Teenagers.* Minneapolis, MN: Winston, 1982.

Dobson, J. *Preparing for Adolescence.* Santa Ana, CA: Vision House, 1978.

Dodson, F. *How to Discipline With Love.* New York: Rawson Associates, 1977.

Drew, N. *Learning the Skills of Peacemaking.* Rolling Hills Estates, CA: Jalmar Press, 1987.

Dyer, W. *What Do You Really Want for Your Children?* New York: William Morrow and Company, Inc., 1985.

Elkind, D. *All Grown Up and No Place to Go.* Reading, MA: Addison-Wesley, 1984.

"Family Fitness: A Complete Exercise Program for Ages Six to Sixty-Plus." *Reader's Digest.* (Special Report) 1987, pp. 2-12.

Fensterheim, H. *Don't Say Yes When You Want to Say No.* New York: Dell Publishing Co., 1975.

Fox, L., and F. Lavin-Weaver. *Unlocking Doors to Self-Esteem.* Rolling Hills Estates, CA: Jalmar Press, 1983.

Freed, A. *TA for Teens.* Rolling Hills Estates, CA: Jalmar Press, 1976.

Freed, A. *TA for Tots,* Revised. Rolling Hills Estates, CA: Jalmar Press, 1991.

Freed, A., and M. Freed. *TA for Kids.* Rolling Hills Estates, CA: Jalmar Press, 1977.

Fugitt, E. D. *He Hit Me Back First!* Rolling Hills Estates, CA: Jalmar Press, 1983.

Gall, M. Synthesis of Research on Teachers' Questioning, *Educational Leadership.* November 1984, pp. 40-47.

Gardner, J. E. *The Turbulent Teens.* Los Angeles: Sorrento Press, Inc., 1983.

Gardner, R. *The Boys' and Girls' Book About Stepfamilies.* New York: Bantam Books, 1982.

Gelb, M. *Present Yourself.* Rolling Hills Estates, CA: Jalmar Press, 1988.

Getzoff, A., and C. McClenahan. *Stepkids: A Survival Guide for Teenagers in Stepfamilies.* New York: Walker and Company, 1984.

Ginott, H. *Teacher and Child.* New York: Avon, 1972.

Gimbel, C. *Why Does Santa Claus Celebrate Christmas?* Rolling Hills Estates, CA: Jalmar Press, 1990.

Greenberg, P. *I Know I'm Myself Because . . .* New York: Human Science Press, 1988.

Gribben, T. *Pajamas Don't Matter.* Rolling Hills Estates, CA: Jalmar Press, 1979.

Harris, T. A. *I'm OK—You're OK.* New York: Avon, 1967.

"Has Rock Gone Too Far?" *People Magazine.* September 16, 1985, pp. 47-53.

Haynes-Klassen. *Learning to Live, Learning to Love.* Rolling Hills Estates, CA: Jalmar Press, 1985.

Hill, W. F. *Learning Through Discussion.* Beverly Hills, CA: Sage Publications, 1977.

Jampolsky, G. G. *Teach Only Love.* New York: Bantam, 1983.

Kalb, J., and Viscott, D. *What Every Kid Should Know.* Boston: Houghton Mifflin, 1974.

Kaufman, R. *Identifying and Solving Problems: A System Approach.* San Diego, CA: University Associates, Inc., 1989.

Kehayan, V. A. *SAGE: Self-Awareness Growth Experiences.* Rolling Hills Estates, CA: Jalmar Press, 1989.

Keirsey, D., and M. Bates. *Please Understand Me.* Del Mar, CA: Prometheus Nemesis, 1978.

Knight, M. E., T. L. Graham, R. A. Juliano, S. R. Miksza, and P. G. Tonnies. *Teaching Children to Love Themselves.* Englewood Cliffs, NJ: Prentice-Hall, 1982.

Kohen-Raz, R. *The Child from 9-13.* Chicago, Illinois: Aldine Adterton, Inc., 1971.

Kreidler, W. *Creative Conflict Resolution: More Than 200 Activities for Keeping Peace in the Classroom.* Glenview, IL: Scott, Foresman and Co., 1984.

Lalli, J. *Feelings Alphabet.* Rolling Hills Estates, CA: Jalmar Press, 1988.

Lansky, D., and S. Dorfman. *How To Survive High School with Minimal Brain Damage.* Minneapolis, MN: Meadowbrook, 1989.

LeShan, E. *What's Going to Happen to Me? When Parents Separate or Divorce.* Four Winds Press, 1978.

Lewis, D., and J. Greene. *Thinking Better.* New York: Rawson, Wade Publishers, Inc., 1982.

Lorayne, H., and J. Lucas. *The Memory Book.* New York: Stein and Day, 1974.

Maslow, A. *Toward a Psychology of Being.* New York: D. Van Nostrand, 1962.

McCabe, M. E., and J. Rhoades. *How to Say What You Mean.* CA: ITA Publications, 1985.

McDaniel, S., and P. Bielen. *Project Self-Esteem.* Rolling Hills Estates, CA: Jalmar Press, 1990.

Miller, G. P. *Teaching Your Child to Make Decisions.* New York: Harper & Row, 1984.

Montessori, M. *The Discovery of the Child.* Notre Dame, IN: Fides, 1967.

Naisbitt, J. *Megatrends.* New York: Warner Books, 1982.

Neufeld, J. *Lisa, Bright and Dark.* New York: S. G. Phillips, 1969.

Newman, M., and B. Berkowitz. *How to Be Your Own Best Friend.* New York: Random House, 1973.

Palmer, P. *Liking Myself.* San Luis Obispo, CA: Impact, 1977.

Palmer, Pat. *The Mouse, the Monster, and Me.* San Luis Obispo, CA: Impact, 1977.

Peal, N. V. *You Can if You Think You Can.* Pawling, NY: Foundation for Christian Living, 1974.

Pelletier, K. *Mind as Healer, Mind as Slayer.* New York: Delacorte, 1977.

Reasoner, Robert, and R. Gilbert. *Building Self-Esteem: Implementation Project Summary.* ERIC Clearinghouse on Counseling and Personnel Services #CG0290, 1988.

Richards, A. K., and I. Willis. *Boy Friends, Girl Friends, Just Friends.* Atheneum, NY: McClelland & Stewart, Ltd., 1979.

Samples, B. *Metaphoric Mind.* Rolling Hills Estates, CA: Jalmar Press, 1991.

Samples, B. *Openmind/Wholemind.* Rolling Hills Estates, CA: Jalmar Press, 1987.

Satir, V. *Peoplemaking.* Palo Alto, CA: Science & Behavior Books Inc., 1972.

Schmuck, R., and P. Schmuck. *A Humanistic Psychology of Education: Making the School Everybody's House.* Palo Alto, CA: Mayfield Publishing Co., 1974.

Schneiderwind, N., and E. Davidson. *Open Minds to Equity: A Sourcebook of Learning Activities to Promote Race, Sex, Class and Age Equity.* NJ: Prentice-Hall, 1983.

Schriner, C. *Feel Better Now.* Rolling Hills Estates, CA: Jalmar Press, 1990.

Sexton, T. G., and D. R. Poling. "Can Intelligence Be Taught?" Bloomingdale, IN: Phi Delta Kappa Educational Foundation, 1973.

Sheehy, G. *Pathfinders,* New York: Morrow, 1981.

Shles, L. *Aliens in My Nest.* Rolling Hills Estates, CA: Jalmar Press, 1988.

Shles, L. *Hoots & Toots & Hairy Brutes.* Rolling Hills Estates, CA: Jalmar Press, 1989.

Shles, L. *Do I Have to Go to School Today?* Rolling Hills Estates, CA: Jalmar Press, 1989.

Shles, L. *Hugs & Shrugs.* Rolling Hills Estates, CA: Jalmar Press, 1987.

Shles, L. *Moths & Mothers/Feathers & Fathers.* Rolling Hills Estates, CA: Jalmar Press, 1989.

Shles, L. *Scooter's Tail of Terror* Rolling Hills Estates, CA: Jalmar Press, 1992.

Silberstein, W. *Helping Your Child Grow Slim.* New York: Simon & Schuster. 1982.

Simpson, B. K. *Becoming Aware of Values.* La Mesa, CA: Pennant Press, 1973.

Skoguland, E. R. *To Anger With Love.* New York: Harper & Row, 1977.

Smith, M. J. *When I Say No I Feel Guilty.* New York: Bantam, 1975.

Stainback, W., and S. Stainback. *How to Help Your Child Succeed in School.* Minneapolis, MN: Meadowbrook, 1988.

Steffenhagen, R.A., and J. D. Burns. *The Social Dynamics of Self-Esteem.* New York, NY: Praeger, 1987.

Steiner, C. *The Original Warm Fuzzy Tale.* Rolling Hills Estates, CA: Jalmar Press, 1977.

"Teenage Fathers." *Psychology Today.* December 1985, pp. 66-70.

Ungerleider, D. *Reading, Writing and Rage.* Rolling Hills Estates, CA: Jalmar Press, 1985.

Viscott, D. *The Language of Feelings.* New York: Pocket Books, 1976.

Vitale, B. M. *Free Flight.* Rolling Hills Estates, CA: Jalmar Press, 1986.

Vitale, B. M. *Unicorns Are Real.* Rolling Hills Estates, CA: Jalmar Press, 1982.

Wahlross, S. *Family Communication.* New York: Macmillan Publishing Co., Inc., 1974.

Warren, N. C. *Make Anger Your Ally.* Garden City, NY: Doubleday 1983.

Wassmer, A. C. *Making Contact.* New York: Dial Press, 1978.

Winn, M. *Children Without Childhood.* New York: Pantheon Books, 1981.

Winter, A., and R. Winter. *Build Your Brain Power.* NY: St. Martin's, 1986.

Wright, E. *Good Morning Class — I Love You!* Rolling Hills Estates, CA: Jalmar Press, 1989.

Wyckoff, J., and B. Unell. *Discipline Without Shouting or Spanking.* Minneapolis, MN: Meadowbrook, 1988.

Young, E. *I Am a Blade of Grass.* Rolling Hills Estates, CA: Jalmar Press, 1989.

Youngs, Bettie B. *Stress in Children: How to Recognize, Avoid and Overcome It.* New York: Avon, 1985.

Youngs, Bettie B. *Helping Your Teenager Deal With Stress. A Survival Guide for Parents and Children.* Los Angeles: Tarcher/St. Martins, 1986.

Youngs, Bettie B. *A Stress Management Guide for Young People.* Rolling Hills Estates, CA: Jalmar Press, 1988.

Youngs, Bettie B. *Goal Setting Skills for Young People.* Rolling Hills Estates, CA: Jalmar Press, 1989.

Youngs, Bettie B. *Problem Solving Skills for Children.* Rolling Hills Estates, CA: Jalmar Press, 1989.

Youngs, Bettie B. *Friendship Is Forever, Isn't It?* Rolling Hills Estates, CA: Jalmar Press, 1990.

Youngs, Bettie B. *Enhancing the Educator's Self-Esteem: It's Your Criteria #1.* Rolling Hills Estates, CA: Jalmar Press, 1992.

Youngs, Bettie B. *The 6 Vital Ingredients of Self-Esteem — How To Develop Them In Your Students.* Rolling Hills Estates, CA, Jalmar Press, 1992.

Youngs, Bettie B. *Stress Management Guide for Educators.* Rolling Hills Estates, CA: Jalmar Press, 1992.

HELP ORGANIZATIONS

Many organizations, some with toll-free 800 phone numbers, provide helpful information; among them:

Alcoholics Anonymous
World Services, Inc.
468 Park Ave. South
New York, NY 10016
(212) 686-1100

Al-Ateen, Al-Anon Family Group Headquarters
P.O. Box 182
New York, NY 10159-0182

Alcoholics Anonymous is an international fellowship of men and women who share the common problem of alcoholism. Family members of alcoholics can receive help through groups associated with Alcoholics Anonymous, mainly Al-Anon and Al-Ateen. Al-Ateen chapters are listed in some phone books or you can contact a local Al-Anon group for more information.

Big Brothers/Big Sisters of America
230 North Thirteenth St.
Philadelphia, PA 19107
(215) 567-7000

Big Brother/Big Sisters of America is a national youth-serving organization based on the concept of a one-to-one relationship between an adult volunteer and an at-risk child, usually from a one-parent family. With more than 495 agencies located nationwide, the organization is dedicated to providing children and youth with adult role models and mentors who help enrich the children's lives, as well as their own, through weekly interaction. Volunteers go through a screening process before being accepted into the program, and professional caseworkers provide assistance, support, and on-going supervision for all matches. Check the white pages of your phone book for the agency nearest you.

Boys' National Hotline
(800) 448-3000 (toll-free)
This hotline provides emergency crisis counseling.

Family Service America (FSA)
11700 West Lake Park Drive
Park Place
Milwaukee, WI 53224
(414) 359-1040

FSA is a membership organization of agencies that deals with family problems, serving more than 1000 communities throughout the United States and Canada. Member agencies serve families and individuals through counseling, advocacy, and family life education. Consult the phone book for the agency nearest you.

National Center for Missing and Exploited Children
2101 Wilson Blvd., Ste. 550
Arlington, VA 22021
(703) 235-3900

The center assists families, citizens' groups, law enforcement agencies, and governmental institutions. The center also has a toll-free number for reporting information that could lead to the location and recovery of a missing child. The number is (800) 843-5678.

National Child Abuse Hotline
P.O. Box 630
Hollywood, CA 90028
(800) 422-4453 (toll-free)

The National Child Abuse Hotline handles crises calls and information and offers referrals to every county in the United States. The hotline is manned by professionals holding a master's degree or Ph.D. in psychology. The hotline also provides literature about child abuse prevention. This program is sponsored by Childhelp USA, which is located in Woodland, CA.

National Clearinghouse for Alcohol and Drug Information (NCADI)
P.O. Box 2345
Rockville, MD 20852
(301) 468-2600
(800) 729-6686 (toll-free)

NCADI is the information component of the Office for Substance Abuse Prevention (OSAP) of the U.S. Dept. of Health and Human Services. The clearinghouse maintains an inventory of hundreds of publications developed by Federal agencies and private-sector organizations. Most publications are free or are available in bulk quantities for a small fee. NCADI also offers fact verification, video loans, dissemination of grant announcements and application kits. NCADI provides access to the Prevention Materials Database, an online computer database designed to help select specific items from the NCADI's collection of prevention materials. NCADI publishes "Prevention Pipeline," a bimonthly publication that contains the latest information about research, resources, and activities within the prevention field.

National Council for Self-Esteem
P.O. Box 277877
Sacramento, CA 95827-7877
(916) 455-NCSE
(916) 454-2000

The NCSE is dedicated to promoting and developing quality self-esteem information. The NCSE's mission is to spread the ethics of self-esteem throughout the United States. The organization seeks to ensure that self-esteem information is readily available to those who seek it. Operating as Self-Esteem Central, the NSCE collects information on the best self-esteem curriculums, school programs, drug prevention programs, drop-out prevention programs, study courses, videos, and audio tape programs. Self-Esteem Central houses the National Self-Esteem Library, reported to be the largest collection of self-esteem resources in the world. The library offers research assistance and audio tape programs. The "Self-Esteem Today" newsletter offers the latest in new ideas to develop self-esteem, including current research, model programs, and upcoming conference information. More than 50 local Self-Esteem Councils exist in 20 states. For more information, or to start a council in your city, write the NSCE.

National Institute on Drug Abuse
P.O. Box 100
Summit, NJ 07901
(800) COCAINE (toll-free)

The National Institute on Drug Abuse hotline is a confidential drug abuse treatment referral service. The hotline provides information on local referrals and help for drug abusers and other concerned individuals.

National Runaway Switch Board
(800) 621-4000 (toll-free)

National Youth Work Alliance
1346 Connecticut Ave., N.W.
Washington, D.C. 20036
Offers local referrals for runaway or teen crisis shelters.

Parents Anonymous (P.A.)
7120 Franklin Ave.
Los Angeles, CA 90046
(800) 421-0353 (toll-free, outside CA)
(800) 352-0386 (toll-free, CA)

P.A. is a self-help program for parents under stress and for abused children. There are no fees and no one is required to reveal his or her name. Group members support and encourage each other in searching out positive alternatives to the abusive behavior in their lives. To locate a P.A. in your area, call the toll-free hotline numbers listed above.

Crisis counseling and information available 24 hours a day, seven days a week.

Stepfamily Association of America, Inc.
215 Centennial Mall South, Suite 212
Lincoln, NE 68508
(402) 477-STEP

Stepfamily Association of America provides education, information, support, and advocacy for stepfamilies. The association publishes a quarterly newsletter, *Stepfamilies*, and the book, *Stepfamilies Stepping Ahead*. Local chapters offer classes, workshops, and support groups for stepfamilies. Members of SAA may attend these meetings at no charge.

Suicide Prevention

Almost every state and major city has one or more suicide hotlines and/or suicide prevention centers. For centers in your area, check with your phone operator, or the State, City, or County Health & Human Services headings in your phone book.

United Way, Inc.

Check the phone book to contact the United Way organization in your area to find the Family Services Agency nearest you. These organizations offer a variety of family counseling services.

Notes to Remember

Notes To Remember

Order NOW 10% Discount On 3 Or More Titles!

20 YEARS AWARD WINNING PUBLISHER

At Last... You Can Be That "MOST MEMORABLE" PARENT/TEACHER/CARE-GIVER To Every Person Whose Life You Touch (Including Your Own!)

HELP KIDS TO: ❖ IMPROVE GRADES ❖ INCREASE CLASS PARTICIPATION ❖ BECOME MORE ATTENTIVE
ENCOURAGE & INSPIRE THEM AND YOU TO: ❖ TACKLE PROBLEMS ❖ ACHIEVE GOALS
AND
IMPROVE SELF-ESTEEM — BOTH THEIRS AND YOURS

Our authors are not just writers, but researchers and practitioners. Our books are not just written, but proven effective. All 100% tested, 100% practical, 100% effective. Look over our titles, choose the ones you want, and send your order today. You'll be glad you did. Just remember, our books are "SIMPLY THE BEST."

Bradley L. Winch, Ph.D., JD — President and Publisher

Sandy Mc Daniel & Peggy Bielen

Project Self-Esteem, Expanded (Gr. K-8)

Innovative *parent involvement program*. Used by over 2000 schools/400,000 participants. Teaches children to respect themselves and others, make sound decisions, honor personal and family value systems, develop vocabulary, attitude, goals and behavior needed for *living successfully*, *practicing responsible behavior* and *avoiding drug and alcohol use*. **VHS, 1½ hrs. $149.95**

0-915190-59-1, 408 pages, **JP-9059-1 $39.95**
8½ x 11, paperback, illus., reprod. act. sheets

Esteem Builders (Gr. K-8)

Teach self-esteem via curriculum content. Best K-8 program available. Uses 5 building blocks of self-esteem (*secuirity/selfhood/affiliation/mission/ competence*) as base. Over 250 grade level/curric. content cross-correlated activities. Also assess. tool, checklist of educator behaviors for modeling, 40 week lesson planner, ext. bibliography and more.

Paperback, 464 pages, **JP-9053-2 $39.95**
Spiral bound, **JP-9088-5 $44.95**, 8½ x 11, illus.

Michele Borba, Ph.D.

NOT JUST AUTHORS BUT RESEARCHERS AND PRACTITIONERS.

Naomi Drew, M.A.

Learning The Skills of Peacemaking: Communicating/Cooperation/Resolving Conflict (Gr. K-8)

Help kids say "No" to fighting. Establish WIN/WIN guidelines for conflicts in your classroom. *Over fifty lessons:* peace begins with me; integrating peacemaking into our lives; exploring our roots and interconnectedness. Great for *self-esteem* and *cultural diversity* programs.

0-915190-46-X, 224 pages, **JP-9046-X $21.95**
8½ x 11, paperback, illus., reprod. act. sheets

6 Vital Ingredients of Self-Esteem: How To Develop Them In Your Students (Gr. K-12)

Put self-esteem to work for your students. Learn practical ways to help kids manage school, make decisions, accept consequences, manage time, and discipline themselves to set worthwhile goals...and much more. *Covers developmental stages from ages 2 to 18, with implications for self-esteem at each stage.*

0-915190-72-9, 192 pages, **JP-9072-9 $19.95**
8½ x 11, paperback, biblio., appendices

NEW

Bettie B. Youngs, Ph.D.

NOT JUST WRITTEN BUT PROVEN EFFECTIVE.

NEW

Bettie B. Youngs, Ph.D.

You & Self-Esteem: The Key To Happiness & Success (Gr. 5-12)

Comprehensive *workbook* for young people. Defines *self-esteem* and its importance in their lives; helps them identify why and how it adds or detracts from their vitality; shows them how to protect it from being shattered by others; outlines a *plan of action* to keep their self-esteem *positive*. Very useful. Companion to *6 Vital Ingredients*.

0-915190-83-4, 160 pages, **JP-9083-4 $16.95**
8½ x 11, paperback, biblio., appendices

Partners for Change: Peer Helping Guide For Training and Prevention (Gr. K-12)

This comprehensive *program guide* provides an excellent *peer support program* for program coordinators, peer leaders, professionals, group homes, churches, social agencies and schools. *Covers 12 areas,* including suicide, HIV / Aids, child abuse, teen pregnancy, substance abuse, low self esteem, dropouts, child abduction. etc.

Paperback, 464 pages, **JP-9069-9 $44.95**
Spiral bound, **JP-9087-7 $49.95**, 8½ x 11, illus.

NEW

V. Alex Kehayan, Ed.D.

100% TESTED — 100% PRACTICAL — 100% GUARANTEED.

V. Alex Kehayan, Ed.D.

Self-Awareness Growth Experiences (Gr. 7-12)

Over *593 strategies/activities* covering affective learning goals and objectives. To increase: self-awareness/self-esteem/social interaction skills/problem-solving, decision-making skills/coping ability /ethical standards/independent functioning/creativity. Great *secondary resource*. Useful in counseling situations.

0-915190-61-3, 224 pages, **JP-9061-3 $16.95**
6 x 9, paperback, illus., 593 activities

Unlocking Doors to Self-Esteem (Gr. 7-12)

Contains *curriculum content objectives with underlying social objectives.* Shows how to teach both at the same time. *Content objectives* in English/Drama/Social Science/Career Education/Science/Physical Education. *Social objectives* in Developing Positive Self-Concepts/Examining Attitudes, Feelings and Actions/Fostering Positive Relationships.

0-915190-60-5, 224 pages, **JP-9060-5 $16.95**
6 x 9, paperback, illus., 100 lesson plans

C. Lynn Fox, Ph.D. & Francine L. Weaver, M.A.

ORDER FROM: B.L. Winch & Associates/Jalmar Press, 45 Hitching Post Drive, Bldg. 2, Rolling Hills Estates, CA 90274-5169
CALL TOLL FREE — (800) 662-9662. • (310) 547-1240 • FAX (310) 547-1644 • Add 10% shipping; $3 minimum

4/92

Order NOW 10% Discount On 3 Or More Titles!

DISCOVER materials for positive self-esteem.
CREATE a positive environment in your classroom or home by opening a world of understanding.

20 YEARS AWARD WINNING PUBLISHER

Good Morning Class - I Love You (Staff)
Contains thought provoking quotes and questions about *teaching from the heart*. Helps love become an integral part of the learning that goes on in every classroom. Great for new teachers and for experienced teachers who sometimes become frustrated by the system. Use this book to begin and end your day. Greet your students every day with: "*Good morning class - I love you.*"

Esther Wright, M.A.

0-915190-58-3, 80 pages, **JP-9058-3 $7.95**
5½ x 8½, paperback, illus./**Button $1.50**

Enhancing Educator's Self-Esteem: It's Criterion #1 (Staff)
For the educator, a *healthy self-esteem* is job criterion No. 1! When high, it empowers us and adds to the vitality of our lives; when low it saps energy, erodes our confidence, lowers productivity and blocks our initiative to care about self and others. Follow the *plan of action* in this great resource to develop your self-esteem.

0-915190-79-6, 144 pages, **JP-9079-6 $16.95**
8½ x 11, paperback

NEW

Bettie B. Youngs, Ph.D.

NOT JUST AUTHORS BUT RESEARCHERS AND PRACTITIONERS.

I Am a Blade of Grass (Staff)
Create a school where all — students, teachers, administrators, and parents — see themselves as both learners and leaders *in partnership*. Develop a new *compact for learning* that focuses on results, that promotes *local initiative* and that *empowers* people at all levels of the system. How to in this *collaborative curriculum*. Great for self-esteem.

Elaine Young, M.A. with R. Frelow, Ph.D.

0-915190-54-0, 176 pages, **JP-9054-0 $14.95**
6 x 9, paperback, illustrations

Stress Management for Educators: A Guide to Manage Our Response to Stress (Staff)
Answers these significant questions for educators: *What is stress?* What causes it? How do I cope with it? What can be done to manage stress to moderate its negative effects? Can stress be used to advantage? How *can educators be stress-proofed* to help them remain at *peak performance?* How do I keep going in spite of it?

0-915190-77-X, 112 pages, **JP-9077-X $12.95**
8½ x 11, paperback, illus., charts

NEW

Bettie B. Youngs, Ph.D.

NOT JUST WRITTEN BUT PROVEN EFFECTIVE.

REVISED

He Hit Me Back First: Self-Esteem Through Self-Discipline (Gr. K-8)
By whose authority does a child choose right from wrong? Here are *activities* directed toward *developing* within the child an *awareness* of his own *inner authority* and ability to choose (will power) and the resulting sense of *responsibility*, freedom and *self-esteem*. 29 seperate activities.

Eva D. Fugitt, M.A.

0-915190-64-8, 120 pages, **JP-9064-8 $12.95**
8½ x 11, paperback, appendix, biblio.

Self-Esteem: The "Affiliation" Building Block (Gr. K-6)
Making friends is *easy* with the activities in this thoroughly researched book. Students are paired, get to know about each other, produce a book about their new *friend*, and present it in class. Exciting activities help discover commonalities. Great *self-esteem booster*. Revised after 10 years of field testing. Over 150 activities in 18 lessons.

0-915190-75-3, 192 pages, **JP-9075-3 $19.95**
8½ x 11, paperback, illustrations, activities

NEW

C. Lynn Fox, Ph.D.

100% TESTED — 100% PRACTICAL — 100% GUARANTEED.

Feel Better Now: 30 Ways to Handle Frustration in Three Minutes or Less (Staff/Personal)
Teaches people to *handle stress as it happens* rapidly and directly. This basic requirement for *emotional survival* and *physical health* can be learned with the methods in this book. Find your own recipe for relief. Foreword: Ken Keyes, Jr. "*A mine of practical help*" — says Rev. Robert Schuller.

Chris Schriner, Rel.D.

0-915190-66-4, 180 pages, **JP-9066-4 $9.95**
6 x 9, paperback, appendix, bibliography

Peace in 100 Languages: A One-Word Multilingual Dictionary (Staff/Personal)
A candidate for the Guinness Book of World Records, it is the *largest/smallest dictionary ever published*. Envisioned, researched and developed by *Russian peace activists*. Ancient, national, local and special languages covered. A portion of purchase price will be donated to joint U.S./Russian peace project. **Peace Button $1.50**

0-915190-74-5, 48 pages, **JP-9074-5 $9.95**
5 x 10, glossy paperback, full color

NEW

By:
M. Kabattchenko,
V. Kochurov,
L. Koshanova,
E. Kononenko,
D. Kuznetsov,
A. Lapitsky,
V. Monakov,
L. Stoupin, and
A. Zagorsky

Shalom • Paz
¡PEACE!
Paix • Vrede

ORDER NOW FOR 10% DISCOUNT ON 3 OR MORE TITLES.

Learning to Live, Learning to Love (Staff/Personal)
Important things are often quite simple. But simple things are not necessarily easy. If you are finding that learning to live and learning to love are at times difficult, you are in good company. People everywhere are finding it a tough challenge. This simple book will help. Shows how to separate "*treasure*" from "*trash*" in our lives.

Joanne Haynes-Klassen

0-915190-38-9, 160 pages, **JP-9038-9 $7.95**
6 x 9, paperback, illustrations

Reading, Writing and Rage (Staff)
An autopsy of one profound *school failure*, disclosing the complex processes behind it and the *secret rage* that grew out of it. Developed from educational therapist's viewpoint. A must reading for anyone working with the *learning disabled*, *functional illiterates* or *juvenile delinquents*. Reads like fiction. Foreword by Bruce Jenner.

0-915190-42-7, 240 pages, **JP-9042-7 $16.95**
5½ x 8½, paperback, biblio., resources

D. Ungerleider, M.A.

ORDER FROM: B.L. Winch & Associates/Jalmar Press, 45 Hitching Post Drive, Bldg. 2, Rolling Hills Estates, CA 90274-5169
CALL TOLL FREE — (800) 662-9662. • (310) 547-1240. • FAX (310) 547-1644 • Add 10% shipping; $3 minimum

4/92

Order NOW 10% Discount On 3 Or More Titles!

DISCOVER books on self-esteem for kids.
ENJOY great reading with Warm Fuzzies and Squib, the adventurous owl.

20 YEARS AWARD WINNING PUBLISHER

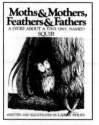

Larry Shles, M.A.

Moths & Mothers/Feathers & Fathers: The Story of Squib, The Owl, Begins (Ages 5-105)

Heartwarming story of a tiny owl who cannot fly or hoot as he learns to put words with his feelings. He faces frustration, grief, fear, guilt and loneliness in his life, just as we do. Struggling with these *feelings*, he searches, at least, for *understanding*. Delightfully illustrated. Ageless.

0-915190-57-5, 72 pages, **JP-9057-5** $7.95
8½ x 11, paperback, illustrations

Hoots & Toots & Hairy Brutes: The Continuing Adventures of Squib, The Owl (Ages 5-105)

Squib, who can only toot, sets out to learn how to give a mighty hoot. Even the *owl-odontist* can't help and he fails completely. Every reader who has struggled with *life's limitations* will recognize his own *struggles* and *triumphs* in the microcosm of Squib's forest world. A parable for all ages.

0-915190-56-7, 72 pages, **JP-9056-7** $7.95
8½ x 11, paperback, illustrations

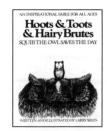

Larry Shles, M.A.

NOT JUST AUTHORS BUT RESEARCHERS AND PRACTITIONERS.

Larry Shles, M.A.

Hugs & Shrugs: The Continuing Saga of Squib, The Owl (Ages 5-105)

Squib feels *lonely*, *depressed* and *incomplete*. His reflection in the pond shows that he has lost a piece of himself. He thinks his missing piece fell out and he searches in vain outside of himself to find it. Only when he discovers that it fell in and not out does he *find inner-peace* and *become whole*. Delightfully illustrated. Ageless.

0-915190-47-8, 72 pages, **JP-9047-8** $7.95
8½ x 11, paperback, illustrations

Aliens in my Nest: Squib Meets the Teen Creature (Ages 5-105)

What does it feel like to face a snarly, surly, defiant and non-communicative older brother turned *adolescent*? Friends, dress code, temperament, entertainment, room decor, eating habits, authority, music, isolation, *internal and external conflict* and many other *areas of change* are *dealt with*. Explores how to handle every situation.

0-915190-49-4, 80 pages, **JP-9049-4** $7.95
8½ x 11, paperback, illustrations

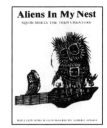

Larry Shles, M.A.

NOT JUST WRITTEN BUT PROVEN EFFECTIVE.

Larry Shles, M.A.

Do I Have to Go to School Today? Squib Measures Up! (Ages 5-105)

Squib *dreads* going to *school*. He day-dreams about all the reasons he has not to go: the school bus will swallow him, the older kids will be mean to him, numbers and letters confuse him, he is too small for sports, etc. But, in the end, he *goes because* his *teacher accepts him "just as he is."* Very esteeming. Great metaphor for all ages.

0-915190-62-1, 64 pages, **JP-9062-1** $7.95
8½ x 11, paperback, illustrations

**Scooter's Tail of Terror
A Fable of Addiction and Hope (Ages 5-105)**

Well-known author and illustrator, Larry Shles, introduces a new forest character — a squirrel named Scooter. He faces the challenge of addiction, but is offered a way to overcome it. As with the Squib books, the story is *simple*, yet the message is *dramatic*. The story touches the child within each reader and *presents the realities of addiction*.

0-915190-89-3, 80 pages, **JP-9089-3** $9.95
8½ x 11, paperback, illustrations

NEW

Larry Shles, M.A.

100% TESTED — 100% PRACTICAL — 100% GUARANTEED.

REVISED

Alvyn Freed, Ph.D.

TA for Tots (and other prinzes) Revised (Gr. PreK-3)

Over 500,000 sold. New upright format. Book has helped thousands of young *children* and their *parents* to better *understand* and *relate* to each other. Helps youngsters realize their *intrinsic worth* as human beings; builds and strengthens their *self-esteem*. *Simple* to understand.
Coloring Book $1.95 / I'm OK Poster $3

0-915190-73-7, 144 pages, **JP-9073-7** $14.95
8½ x 11, paperback, delightful illustrations

TA for Kids (and grown-ups too) (Gr. 4-9)

Over 250,000 sold. An ideal book to help youngsters *develop self-esteem*, esteem of others, *personal and social responsibility*, critical thinking and independent judgment. Book recognizes that each person is a unique human being with the capacity to learn, grow and develop. Hurray for TA! Great for parents and other care givers.

0-915190-09-5, 112 pages, **JP-9009-5** $9.95
8½ x 11, paperback, illustrations

Alvyn Freed, Ph.D.
& Margaret Freed

ORDER NOW FOR 10% DISCOUNT ON 3 OR MORE TITLES.

Alvyn Freed, Ph.D.

TA for Teens (and other important people) (Gr. 8-12)

Over 100,000 sold. The book that tells teenagers they're OK! Provides help in growing into adulthood in a mixed-up world. Contrasts freedom and irresponsibility with knowing that *youth need* the *skill*, *determination* and *inner strength* to reach *fulfillment* and *self-esteem*. No talking down to kids, here.

0-915190-03-6, 258 pages, **JP-9003-6** $18.95
8½ x 11, paperback, illustrations

The Original Warm Fuzzy Tale (Gr. Pre K-Adult)

Over 100,000 sold. The concept of Warm Fuzzies and Cold Pricklies originated in this delightful story. A *fairy tale* in every sense, *with* adventure, fantasy, heroes, villians and a *moral*. Children (and adults, too) will enjoy this beautifully illustrated book. **Songs of Warm Fuzzy Cass. $12.95. Warm Fuzzies, JP-9042 $0.99 each.**

0-915190-08-7, 48 pages, **JP-9008-7** $7.95
6 x 9, paperback, full color illustrations

Claude Steiner, Ph.D

ORDER FROM: B.L. Winch & Associates/Jalmar Press, 45 Hitching Post Drive, Bldg. 2, Rolling Hills Estates, CA 90274-5169
CALL TOLL FREE — (800) 662-9662. • (310) 547-1240. • FAX (310) 547-1644 • Add 10% shipping; $3 minimum

Order NOW 10% Discount On 3 Or More Titles!

OPEN your mind to wholebrain thinking and creative parenting.
GROW by leaps and bounds with our new ways to think and learn.

20 YEARS AWARD WINNING PUBLISHER

Openmind/Wholemind: Parenting and Teaching Tomorrow's Children Today (Staff/Personal)

Can we learn to *treat* the *brain/mind system* as *open* rather than closed? Can we learn to *use* all our *learning modalities, learning styles, creativities* and *intelligences* to create a product far greater than the sum of its parts? Yes! This primer for parents and teachers shows how.

Bob Samples, M.A. 0-915190-45-1, 272 pages, **JP-9045-1 $14.95**
7 x 10, paperback, 81 B/W photos, illust.

Unicorns Are Real: A Right-Brained Approach to Learning (Gr. K-Adult)

Over 100,000 sold. The *alternate methods* of *teaching/learning* developed by the author have helped literally thousands of children and adults with *learning difficulties*. A book of *simple ideas* and *activities* that are easy to use, yet dramatically effective. Video of techniques also available: **VHS, 1½ hrs., JP-9113-0 $149.95. Unicorn Poster $4.95.**

0-915190-35-4, 144 pages, **JP-9035-4 $12.95**
8½ x 11, paperback, illus., assessment

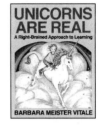

Barbara Meister Vitale, M.A.

NOT JUST AUTHORS BUT RESEARCHERS AND PRACTITIONERS.

REVISED

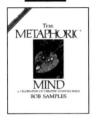

Metaphoric Mind: A Celebration of Creative Consciousness (Revised) (Staff/Personal)

A plea for a balanced way of thinking and being in a culture that stands on the knife-edge between *catastrophe* and *transformation*. The metaphoric mind is *asking* again, quietly but insistently, *for equilibrium*. For, after all, equilibrium is the way of nature. A revised version of a classic.

Bob Samples, M.A. 0-915190-68-0, 272 pages, **JP-9068-0 $16.95**
7 x 10, paperback, B/W photos, illus.

Free Flight: Celebrating Your Right Brain (Staff/Personal)

Journey with Barbara Meister Vitale, from her uncertain childhood perceptions of being *"different"* to the acceptance and adult celebration of that difference. A how to book *for right-brained people in a left-brained world*. Foreword by Bob Samples- *"This book is born of the human soul."* Great gift item for your right-brained friends.

0-915190-44-3, 128 pages, **JP-9044-3 $9.95**
5½ x 8½, paperback, illustrations

Barbara Meister Vitale, M.A.

NOT JUST WRITTEN BUT PROVEN EFFECTIVE.

NEW

Imagine That! Getting Smarter Through Imagery Practice (Gr. K-Adult)

Understand and *develop* your own *seven intelligences* in only minutes a day. Help children do the same. The results will amaze you. Clear, step-by-step ways show you how to create your own imagery exercises for any area of learning or life and how to *relate imagery* exercises *to curriculum content*.

Lane Longino Waas, Ph.D. 0-915190-71-0, 144 pages, **JP-9071-0 $12.95**
6 x 9, paperback, 42 B/W photos, biblio.

Becoming Whole (Learning) Through Games (Gr. K-Adult)

New ideas for old games. *Develop* your *child's brain power, motivation* and *self-esteem by playing*. An excellent parent/ teacher guide and skills checklist to 100 standard games. Included are auditory, visual, motor, directional, modality, attention, educational, social and memory skills. Great resource for care givers.

0-915190-70-2, 288 pages, **JP-9070-2 $16.95**
6 x 9, paperback, glossary, biblio.

NEW

Gwen Bailey Moore, Ph.D. & Todd Serby

100% TESTED — 100% PRACTICAL — 100% GUARANTEED.

Present Yourself: Great Presentation Skills (Staff/Personal)

Use *mind mapping* to become a presenter who is a dynamic part of the message. Learn about transforming fear, knowing your audience, setting the stage, making them remember and much more. *Essential reading* for anyone interested in *communication*. This book will become the standard work in its field. **Hardback, JP-9050-8 $16.95**

Michael J. Gelb, M.A. 0-915190-51-6, 128 pages, **JP-9051-6 $9.95**
6 x 9, paperback, illus., mind maps

The Two Minute Lover (Staff/Personal)

With wit, wisdom and compassion, "The Two-Minute Lovers" and their proteges guide you through the steps of *building* and *maintaining* an *effective relationship* in a *fast-paced world*. They offer encouragement, inspiration and practical techniques for living happily in a relationship, even when outside pressures are enormous. Done like the "One Minute Manager".

0-915190-52-4, 112 pages, **JP-9052-4 $9.95**
6 x 9, paperback, illustrations

Asa Sparks, Ph.D.

ORDER NOW FOR 10% DISCOUNT ON 3 OR MORE TITLES.

The Turbulent Teens: Understanding Helping, Surviving (Parents/Counselors)

Come to grips with the difficult issues of rules and the limits of parental tolerance, recognizing the necessity for *flexibility* that takes into consideration changes in the adolescent as well as the imperative *need for control*, agreed upon *expectations* and *accountability*. A must read! Useful in counseling situations.

James E. Gardner, Ph.D. 0-913091-01-4, 224 pages, **JP-9101-4 $8.95**
6 x 9, paperback, case histories

The Parent Book: Raising Emotionally Mature Children - Ages 3-15 (Parents)

Improve *positive bonding* with your child in five easy steps: *listen* to the feelings; *learn* the basic concern; *develop* an action plan; *confront* with support; *spend* 1 to 1 time. Ideas for helping in 4 *self-esteem* related areas: *awareness; relating; competence; integrity*. 69 sub-catagories. Learn what's missing and what to do about it.

0-915190-15-X, 208 pages, **JP-9015-X $9.95**
8½ x 11, paperback, illus., diag/Rx.

Howard Besell, Ph.D. & Thomas P. Kelly, Jr.

ORDER FROM: B.L. Winch & Associates/Jalmar Press, 45 Hitching Post Drive, Bldg. 2, Rolling Hills Estates, CA 90274-5169
CALL TOLL FREE — (800) 662-9662. • (310) 547-1240 • FAX (310) 547-1644 • Add 10% shipping; $3 minimum